GCSE Applied Business

Portfolio Book

Rob Jones ✪ Carlo Raffo ✪ Dave Gray
Edited by Ian Chambers

Causeway Press Ltd

Note to students, teachers and lecturers

Students should ALWAYS check with a teacher or lecturer BEFORE starting any portfolio work or investigations. The teacher can then supervise the work and protect the student when carrying out questionnaires or interviews or using the Internet or email for example. Contacts with all people and business organisations should ALWAYS be made through the teacher.

Cover design by Caroline Waring-Collins
Image provided by Getty Images
Graphics by Caroline Waring-Collins and Tim Button
Cartoons by Alan Fraser
Photography by Andrew Allen, Dave Gray, Ian McAnulty
Page design by Caroline Waring-Collins
Reader - Mike Kidson

British Library Cataloguing in Publication Data
A catalogue record of this book is available from the British Library

ISBN 1-902796-63-2

Causeway Press Limited
PO Box 13, Ormskirk, Lancashire, L39 5HP

First impression 2003

Design and page origination by Caroline Waring-Collins (Waring-Collins Limited)
Printed and bound by Legoprint, Italy.

Acknowledgements

The publishers and authors would like to thank the following for the use of photographs and other material in this book.
Digital Vision p.5(b),8,32(c),35,39(r),47,58; EasyJet p.21(t); Jerry Bergman/Rex Features p.12; New Mind p20; Photodisc p.5(t),6(b),17(tl),32(t, bl),44,63(t); Ryanair p.21(b); Stockbyte p.17(tr,b),32(br),39(l),51,63(b).
All other material is acknowledged at source.
Thanks also to staff and students at Whalley Range 11-18 High School, Mark Roche, Edge Hill College of Higher Education.

Preface

GCSE Applied Business *Portfolio Book* is designed for students, teachers and lecturers who are following the **GCSE Applied Business (Double Award)** qualification. It gives essential guidance and practice in the skills required to complete the portfolio for Unit 1 (Investigating business) and Unit 2 (People and business). It is divided into 17 short four page sections, each concentrating on a particular topic.

Also available to complement this book.

- **GCSE Applied Business** - a main course textbook for **GCSE Applied Business (Double Award)** providing comprehensive coverage of the knowledge and skills required for Unit 1 (Investigating business), Unit 2 (People and business) and Unit 3 (Business finance).
- **GCSE Applied Business Teachers' Guide** - a photocopiable guide for teachers which contains suggested answers to all questions in the students' books and important support material.

Contents

1 What is a portfolio for GCSE Applied Business?

What is a portfolio?

A PORTFOLIO is a set of pieces of work gathered together to show your ability. Art students have a portfolio of their paintings. Photographers have a portfolio of their photographs. As a GCSE Applied Business student you have to produce a portfolio of the best work you have done in parts of the course. Your Applied Business portfolio may include examples of the following types of work that you have done.

- Descriptions of businesses that you have visited.
- Notes on different business terms and ideas that you have learnt and used.
- Results from research that you have carried out about businesses.
- Questionnaires and interviews that you have designed.
- Graphs, tables and diagrams showing the findings you have discovered.
- Pictures and illustrations which show how a business works.
- Summaries and conclusions that you have written about a business.

All work and investigations which you are planning for your portfolio must be supervised and approved by your teacher before you begin.

Why produce a portfolio?

In Applied Business you will need to produce a portfolio for Unit 1 and Unit 2 of the course. Unit 1 is Investigating business and Unit 2 is People and business. Together these units make up two-thirds of your course. The Portfolio is used to assess your knowledge, understanding and skills for those two Units. For Unit 3, Business Finance, your knowledge, understanding and skills are assessed by a written examination. In Applied Business therefore two-thirds of your marks are gained from the portfolio and only one-third from an exam.

There are advantages to being assessed by portfolio.

- You have much more time to complete the work.
- You can use notes and research to help you write the portfolio.
- You can ask advice of your teachers and friends about how to improve your portfolio.
- You can use IT to help improve the presentation and spelling of your work.
- Once you have handed it in and it has been assessed, you will know how well you are doing in the course.
- You will have finished your portfolio long before any great rush of exams.

Practise your skills

Which of the following pieces of work might you include in your Applied Business portfolio?

(a) A bar chart showing the different ages of people who might buy a product you are researching.

(b) A handout your teacher has given you on different types of business organisation.

(c) Your own notes on the different types of business organisation.

(d) A photocopy of a chapter from a Business textbook.

(e) A written summary of your conclusions about a business.

What has to be in your Applied Business portfolio? Unit 1 - Investigating business

You will need to produce a portfolio based upon your investigation of two contrasting businesses. These businesses have to be different.

For example, you might choose a large and a small business to compare or a manufacturer and a service provider. Small businesses might be sole traders, with one owner. Examples might be people offering services such as plumbers, hairdressers, electricians or car mechanics, small retailers, or craftspeople and manufacturers in small workshops making furniture, components or other products. Or they might be partnerships with just two or a few partners, such as solicitors, accountants or designers.

Large businesses might be private or public limited companies manufacturing products or offering services.

For your Unit 1 portfolio, you will need to find out about the following.

- What each business does, its aims and objectives, the type of ownership and the location.
- The purposes and activities of each functional area.
- How the different businesses communicate.
- External influences, including competitors, location and environment.

For Unit 1 you are researching a wide range of business functions and influences. You then have to compare what you find in two quite different businesses.

Practise your skills

Which of the following combination of businesses might be most useful to use for Unit 1 of the portfolio?

(a) A small corner shop compared with Sainsbury's.
(b) McDonald's compared with Burger King.
(c) British Aerospace compared with a local engineering company.
(d) Your school compared with the local library.

What has to be in your Applied Business portfolio? Unit 2 - People and business

You will need to produce a portfolio based on your investigation of one medium to large business. The business will probably need to be a private limited or a public limited company. These businesses will be large enough to include many of the features about people in business that you are interested in investigating.

For your Unit 2 portfolio, you will need to find out about the following.

- The importance of stakeholders.
- Job roles and contracts of employment.
- Employer and employee rights and responsibilities and how the business deals with disputes.
- Employee recruitment.
- Development and training.
- Customer service and customer protection.

For Unit 2 you are researching the way employees are supported and treated at work in some detail, but this time only in one business.

Practise your skills

Which of the following might you need to investigate for Unit 2?
(a) The methods of production used by businesses.
(b) How an oil company helps its employees to become more skilled by better training.
(c) How a change in interest rates affects a small manufacturer.
(d) How a limited company recruits its employees.

How do you create a portfolio?

For each Unit you will be given a number of tasks to carry out by your teacher. Or you may have to plan out the tasks yourself. By completing the tasks you will be able to build up a report, a written summary of all the information you have collected. This will form the basis for your portfolio for each unit.

- For Unit 1 your portfolio has to cover two different businesses and may be presented as two separate reports.
- For Unit 2 your portfolio only has to cover one business and therefore might just be one report.

In putting together your portfolio for either Unit you will need to follow a number of steps.

Make a summary of the tasks you have to carry out

↓

Produce an action plan showing the time you are going to take for each task so that you will complete the portfolio on time

↓

Carry out all the research you need to be able to complete the tasks

↓

Gather the information together and sort it out so that you can use it

↓

Write what you need for each task, perhaps in draft form to start with, so that you can make changes

↓

Review what you have written against the tasks and what is being assessed, and ask your teacher to look at it as well

↓

Make any improvements that are suggested and produce a final version using IT where possible to improve presentation

↓

Organise your portfolio into a report format with a contents page, an introduction, different sections, a conclusion and a list of sources you have used, and number the pages

↓

Store your work carefully in a file until you have to hand it in to your teacher

key terms

Portfolio - *the collection of evidence you need to present to show your understanding and skills in a subject.*

key terms key terms key terms key terms key terms key terms ke

portfolio practice

Your teacher has asked you to research information while you are on your work experience for your portfolio for Unit 2.

(a) What specific information might you be able to gather from a business to help you with your portfolio?

(b) How would you explain to your supervisor why you are collecting this information?

2 Action planning and time management

What is an action plan?

Planning is important when preparing and writing material for your portfolio. It will help to make it better. An ACTION PLAN might be used. This is a written outline of what must be done to organise an event or complete an assignment. The action plan below was used to complete a written assignment about Cassocks plc, a manufacturer of plastic products.

Action plan

Objective

Write an account describing the main business activities of Cassocks plc

Deadline

24.10.03

Tasks

	Task	Complete by
1.	Obtain the address of Cassocks plc from the Internet.	14.10.03
2.	Write a letter to Cassocks plc asking for an information pack.	14.10.03
3.	Wait for the pack to arrive.	20.10.03
4.	Make notes from information in the pack.	20.10.03
5.	List the order of points that will be made in the account.	21.10.03
6.	Word process the account using the notes.	22.10.03
7.	Correct errors and make changes where necessary.	23.10.03

Review

Couldn't use the Internet due to technical difficulties. There was a two day delay sending out the letter. Allow for computer delays next time.

The aim of the action plan is stated clearly at the beginning.

A list of individual tasks needed to complete the assignment.

A planned deadline for each task will help the final deadline to be met.

Comments on the success of the plan will help to improve future planning.

Practise your skills

List the tasks that might be needed to draw a map showing all the businesses within a mile of your school.

Stages in action planning

The diagram below shows the steps that can be used when action planning. They follow an order. You should discuss your plan with your teacher before you begin for their approval.

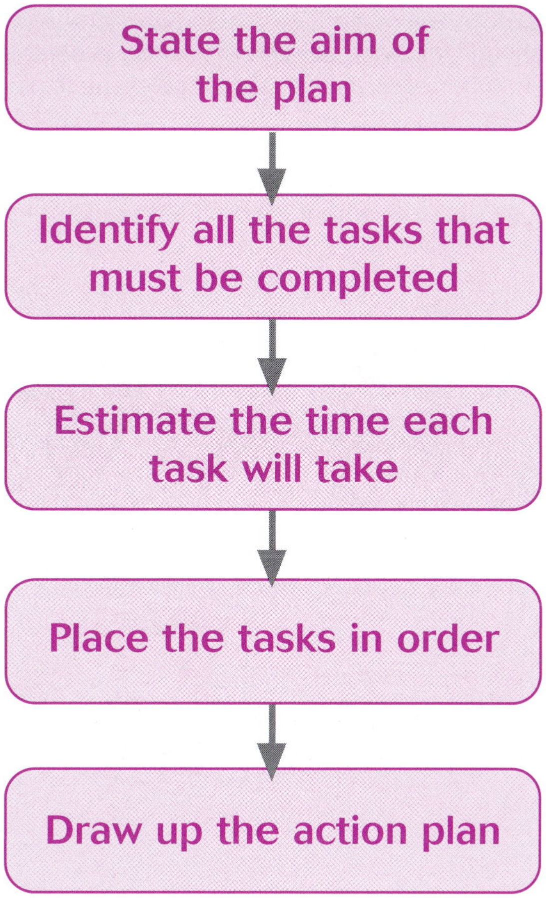

- The aim of the plan must be clear. Examples in your portfolio might be to write a report, plan research or organise a visit.
- Assignments can be broken down into a series of smaller tasks. They should be identified and listed. For example, seven separate tasks are listed when completing the action plan for finding out about the activities of Cassocks plc.
- You can calculate how long it will take to complete an assignment by estimating the time each task will take. Deadlines could also be set for each task.
- Tasks need to be completed in a particular order. For example, you cannot analyse a set of accounts until you have received them.
- The final stage is to write up your action plan. It can be used as a checklist when completing the assignment.

Practise your skills

The following tasks are needed to organise a visit to a local business by your teacher for your class.

- *Write a letter of thanks.*
- *Telephone to make an appointment.*
- *Decide which business to visit.*
- *Decide when you can go.*
- *Prepare for the visit by writing a list of questions to ask.*

Place them in the order you think that they should be carried out.

Why is planning important?

When you throw a party you want it to be successful. So you will plan it. If the party is well planned things are less likely to go wrong and people will enjoy themselves.

Planning the work for your portfolio will make it better and improve your grade.

- It will force you to look ahead. This will help you to identify problems before they arise.
- Planning will reduce the number of mistakes made. For example, you are less likely to overlook important tasks.
- You are more likely to meet the deadline. You will work out how long it takes to finish the assignment and therefore allow enough time for its completion.
- Less time will be wasted. If your assignment is completed quickly there will be more time for other things.

The DOs and DON'Ts of action planning

DOs

- ✔ Stick to your plan. There is little point in producing an action plan if you ignore it.
- ✔ Allow enough time for each task.
- ✔ Allow some time for unexpected problems.
- ✔ Learn from your mistakes.
- ✔ Review your action plan. Reviewing will help improve your planning.

DON'Ts

- ✘ Do not make plans that are impossible to achieve. If you do not achieve them you might start to lose interest and motivation.
- ✘ Do not spend too much time writing your action plan. It is the planning that is important not the plan itself.

Practise your skills

You are going to take a photograph of the inside of a business. List three problems that might arise if this is not planned.

Time management

When working on your portfolio you will have to organise your time effectively. This is called TIME MANAGEMENT.

Time management is an important part of planning. It involves setting out a timetable of activities or tasks and sticking to it. Managing time has a number of benefits.

- It helps you to make sure that deadlines are met on time.
- It helps you to avoid stress.
- It reduces time wasting.
- It might motivate you to work better.
- It can help you to produce more work of a better standard.

Tips on time management

- Draw up a daily timetable. List all activities and tasks including recreation, eating and sleeping. Use your action plans to help draw up the timetable.
- Complete important tasks before those that are less important. This is called prioritising tasks.
- Some tasks must be done first or others are not able to be completed.
- Plan to do the most difficult tasks when you feel at your best. This might be at the start or end of the day, at the weekend or in the week, before or after eating.
- Give yourself plenty of breaks. Do not work for more than one hour without a break.
- Cross off tasks when they are done. You can also give yourself rewards.

Practise your skills

Draw up a timetable for your tasks and activities tomorrow. Start it from the minute you get up in the morning and account for your time in half hour units. Use it and see if you can stick to it.

key terms

***Action plan** - a written document that outlines how a particular aim will be achieved.*
***Time management** - organising time in such a way that it is used effectively.*

key terms key terms key terms key terms key terms key terms ke

portfolio practice

You have been asked to describe the health and safety policy of a company. Draw up an action plan to show how you would do this. You have been given two weeks for this task. Think about:

- what is your objective;
- how long you have;
- the order in which you will carry out tasks;
- what you will do after drawing up the plan.

3 Questionnaires

What is a questionnaire?

A questionnaire is a list of questions that have been written down. Questionnaires are used to collect information. Here are some examples of different types of questions. They have been written for customers of McDonald's.

Question 1

How often do you eat at McDonald's? Please tick one box.

- ☐ Once a week
- ☐ Once a month
- ☐ Once every 6 months
- ☐ Once a year
- ☐ Hardly ever

Question 2

Please give McDonald's a score from 1 to 5 for the following. 1 is poor and 5 is excellent.

- ☐ Food
- ☐ Drink
- ☐ Speed of service
- ☐ Cleanliness
- ☐ Price

Question 3

Circle your favourite burger

Big Mac   Hamburger   Cheeseburger

Question 4

What meal do you usually buy at McDonald's? Include everything, for example drinks, main meal, dips (sauce) and dessert.

____

____

Question 5

What fast food restaurant do you like best and why (for example McDonald's, KFC, Burger King)?

____

____

____

Closed questions

Closed questions give a number of different answers to choose from.

Questions 1, 2 and 3 on the McDonald's questionnaire are closed questions.

Open questions

Open questions allow a person to write their own answer in their own way.

Questions 4 and 5 on the McDonald's questionnaire are open questions.

Practise your skills

Write down:
- *a closed question;*
- *an open question;*

for customers using a video/DVD rental shop.

Why should you use closed questions?

The answers to closed questions are simple to put into numbers. These can be added up easily. For example, 20 people were asked Question 3 of the McDonald's questionnaire. 10 chose a Big Mac as their favourite burger, 6 chose a Cheeseburger and 4 chose a Hamburger. These figures can be shown as percentages.

Big Mac $\frac{10}{20} \times 100 = 50\%$

Cheeseburger $\frac{6}{20} \times 100 = 30\%$

Hamburger $\frac{4}{20} \times 100 = 20\%$

They can also be used to draw bar charts and pie charts.

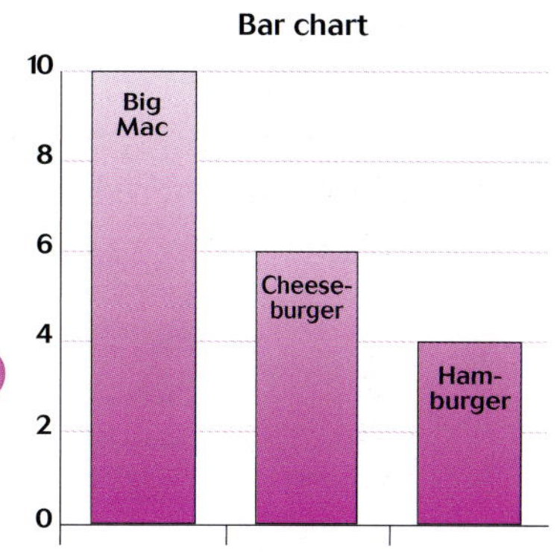

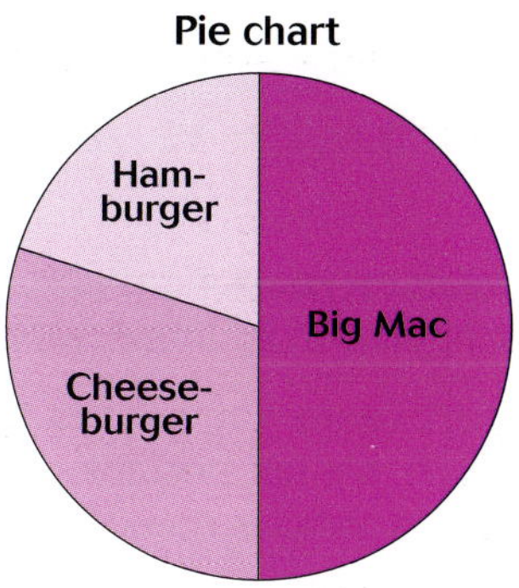

With closed questions, people can only choose from answers that are given. For example, in Question 3 they cannot choose a Bacon McDouble. But they can give their own choice if you add:

Other (please specify) ....

Why should you use open questions?

Open questions let people say whatever they want. They do not have to choose from answers that are given. Open questions can be used when the answer is complicated or when many different answers are possible. For example, there are many reasons why a person might prefer Burger King to McDonald's. An open question might be better than a closed question to find this out.

The DOs and DON'Ts of questionnaires

DOs

- ✔ Test your questionnaire before you use it to make sure it works.
- ✔ Write questions clearly and simply.
- ✔ Make sure the questions mean the same thing to everyone who answers them.
- ✔ Keep the questionnaire as short as you can. People might rush a long questionnaire or might not complete it.
- ✔ Explain the purpose of the questionnaire. People will be more likely to fill it in.

DON'Ts

- ✘ Do not include technical terms. People might not know what they mean.
- ✘ Do not ask leading questions. These are questions which encourage people to give a certain answer. For example, 'Why do you think the manager is doing a good job?' leads people to think the manager is doing a good job.
- ✘ Do not ask questions that have no connection with people's lives.

Practise your skills

What problems with questionnaires does each cartoon show?

Who should be given the questionnaire?

Sometimes you will be able to get answers from all the people you want. For example, you might only need two or three people to fill in a questionnaire in a small business.

In other cases you will not be able to give a questionnaire to everyone you are interested in. For example, it's not possible to give a questionnaire to every McDonald's customer. So you will have to choose a smaller number of people to study. This smaller number is called a SAMPLE.

Choosing a sample

Your sample should reflect the group you are studying. This lets you say that the results of the questionnaire probably apply to all McDonald's customers. What if you want the views of students in your school or college on McDonald's? How might you choose a sample?

Random sampling

A random sample is based on chance, like drawing numbers out of a hat. You could get a list of all students and give each one a number. Then ask your Maths teacher for a table of random numbers. Choose as many numbers as you want from the list. The students with these numbers will make up the sample.

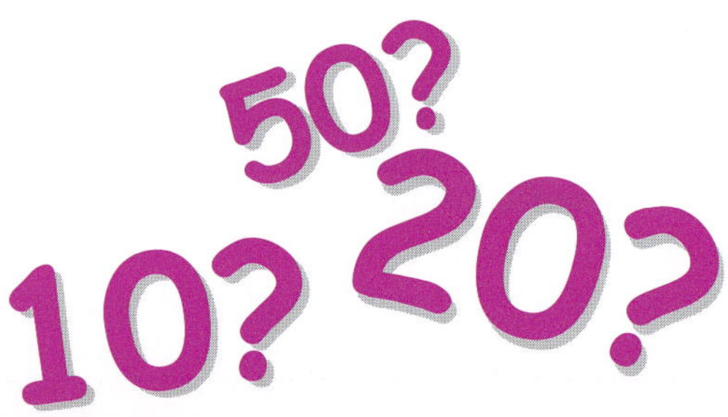

Snowball sampling

Snowball sampling is like rolling a snowball. It gets bigger as you go along. First, decide how many people you want in your sample. Then find a person who visits McDonald's. Ask that person to find someone else who goes to McDonald's, and so on, until the sample is complete.

Quota sampling

This is where the percentage of people you choose for the sample is the same percentage as all people you want to find out about. So if around half of all McDonald's customers are under 25 years old, half of your sample should be under 25.

Practise your skills

How would you choose a sample of people visiting a local leisure centre?

key terms

Closed questions **- *questions where the answer is chosen from a set of alternatives.***
Open questions **- *questions which allow any answer to be given.***
Sample **- *a selection of people from a larger group of people. The sample should reflect the larger group.***

key terms key terms key terms

Tips for questionnaires

Tip 1 Get your teacher's approval before giving out the questionnaire.

Tip 2 When giving out the questionnaire, make sure people know:

- who you are
- what school or college you go to
- what course you are doing
- what the questionnaire is for
- that the answers are confidential.

Tip 3 Decide whether the questionnaire will be:

- given out so that people can answer it in their own time or
- read out to people and their answers written down at the time.

Tip 4 If the questionnaire is given out, arrange a time, place and date to collect it.

Tip 5 Always thank the people who have completed the questionnaire.

portfolio practice

Write a questionnaire to find out employees' views about the business they work in and what motivates them.

Before you write your questionnaire, decide what business you are going to research and who you are going to give your questionnaire to. It might be a friend, a member of the family or someone you know who works for a well known business.

When writing your questions you might take into account the views of employees about:

- the nature of their job;
- how they are rewarded;
- their relations with management;
- their relations with other workers;
- what they like most or least about the business;
- what might make them work harder;
- what might cause them to leave;
- their chance of promotion, training or other ways of improving their position in the business;
- how their job or the business could be improved;
- how long they want to stay in the business.

4 Interviews

What is an interview?

When gathering information for your portfolio you will meet people who are involved in business. You can get information by asking them to answer questions. This is an INTERVIEW.

- Structured interviews ask people to answer a set of prepared questions, which might be written down on a questionnaire.
- In-depth interviews are longer 'chats', where the person answering the questions is asked to give detailed answers and express their views.

You might decide to ask all the questions yourself. This means that you can decide exactly what information you want to be given. If you carry out an interview with a small group of friends, you might feel more confident and the interview might be more interesting if several people ask questions.

What is the purpose of an interview?

An interview will allow you to gather specific information. So you can find out things that you are particularly interested in. Also, some of the information you want might not be available anywhere else. For example, you might want to find out what a local business owner thinks might happen to the business in future. This is best done by interviewing the owner. Or you might interview your family and friends to find out about the business's service. Interviews can also:

- allow you to respond to the answers given, which might give better information;
- reduce the amount of time spent searching for information;
- build links because you may contact the person again for more information;
- develop your oral communication skills;
- build your confidence when dealing with others.

Practise your skills

Look at the list of information below.
1. The accounts of a public limited company.
2. The number of staff employed by a public limited company.
3. The feelings of a customer about the after-sales service of a business.
4. A list of products sold by a mail order company.
Which information might best be gathered using an interview?

Who might you interview?

You may wish to interview a variety of people. Your choice of person will depend on what sort of information you need. Below are some examples. They may help you to choose the right person depending on what you want to find out.

Interview

Business owners or shareholders

Information

Reasons for setting up.
Aims and objectives.
Business organisation.
Liability of owners.
Reason for location.

Customers

Information

Examples of customer services.
Quality of customer services.
Effects of marketing.
Views on price, promotion, product and place.

Office workers

Information

Wages and conditions.
Health & safety issues.
Organisation structure.
Communication methods.

Company accountants

Information

Financial performance.
Financial documents, such as a balance sheet and profit and loss account.

Other businesses and organisations

Health and safety inspectors.
Quality inspectors.
Government bodies.

Human resources manager

Information

Recruitment procedures.
Communication methods.
Training details.
Conditions of employment.

Factory or production workers

Information

Wages and conditions.
Health & safety issues.
Organisation structure.
Communication methods.
Views about their work.

Practise your skills

Look at the list of information below.
1. An overview of the main activities of a business.
2. The system used to attract and select new staff.
3. Details of the main competitors.
4. How IT is used in production.
Who might you choose to interview to find out each of the details above?

How to prepare for an interview

You will get a lot more out of an interview if you are well prepared. The diagram here shows the steps that could be followed when making preparations.

Interviews with business people can be carried out during visits arranged to a business by your teacher. Your teacher should always make the first contact. You can also interview your family and friends who will be customers, employees and business owners. **You must always check with your teacher first if you are planning to arrange an interview. They will advise you on the steps that must be taken to protect your safety and security.**

Choose the right person
The right person will depend on what information you are trying to gather, eg you could interview someone who uses a product if you want to know about customers' views or a production manager to find out how it is made.

Make an appointment through your teacher
Arrange a time and place for the interview.

Draw up a list of questions
Take the list of questions with you. Make sure you have plenty. Ask politely for any other useful information.

Decide how you will record the answers
Will you make notes or use a questionnaire? Will you record the interview?

Write up the results as soon as you return
Write up the information gathered from the interview straight away. It will be easier while it is fresh in your mind.

Types of question

You need to keep the interview flowing once it has begun. This means you will need plenty of questions to ask. The interview would not be successful if you had nothing more to ask after a minute. The following questions might be asked if you were interviewing an office worker about their use of IT.

1. How many hours a day do you spend on the computer?
2. When do you use emails?
3. What do you use the Internet for?
4. Do you use spreadsheets? If so, what for?
5. Describe the IT training that you have received.
6. Can you use IT for personal use? If so, what for?
7. What documents do you write using IT?
8. Describe other applications that you use.
9. How often does your system break down?
10. Do you enjoy using IT at work?

Practise your skills

Write down six questions that you might use when interviewing the owners of small businesses about their objectives in running the businesses.

Recording information from interviews

You will not remember everything that was said during an interview. Therefore you must keep a record. This can be done in a number of ways.

- Make a tape recording of a face to face conversation. You must get permission to do this.
- Use a questionnaire. You could tick answers easily in boxes.
- Make brief notes. Do not try to write down every word the person says. Just try to make a note of the main points.
- Use email or the Internet. This gives a record of the interview on computer. **You must always get permission to use the computer in this way from your teacher**. They will help you to make sure that your security is protected when communicating in this way.
- Carry out an interview over the telephone and record the answers. **Again you must always get permission from a teacher**.
- You might be able to video the interview if permission is given.

Tips when conducting an interview

- Check with your teacher that the person you have chosen to interview is suitable.
- Act professionally. You are representing your school and yourself.
- Always arrive on time.
- Dress smartly. You want to make a good impression.
- Introduce yourself and explain the purpose of the interview.
- Be thoroughly prepared with your questions.
- Encourage the person to talk so that you get the information you need.
- Don't waste people's time. Plan how long the interview will last, ie between 15 -30 minutes.
- Remember to write and thank the person you interviewed.

key terms

Interview *- where someone is asked to answer questions by an interviewer to find out information or the person's opinions.*

portfolio practice

You are preparing to interview a parent, relative, teacher or a friend. You are going to ask them about their views on the prices, marketing and competition of a product that they buy. Write a list of 10-15 questions that you might ask before the interview.

5 Using the Internet and email

Finding business information on the Internet

The Internet is a very powerful source of information. Most large and medium sized businesses have their own websites. So will many small businesses. There are also many other websites that might provide useful business information.

The first page on a website is known as the home page. It's like a contents page in a book. The home page shown below is for New Mind, an Internet design company. There is a set of choices. If you click on 'Profile' you will be given another set of choices (overview, values, history and awards). By clicking onto various links you will eventually find what you are looking for. Most sites operate in a similar way to this. But one site might not operate in exactly the same way as another. Also, a website might be redesigned so it could operate differently if you return at a later date.

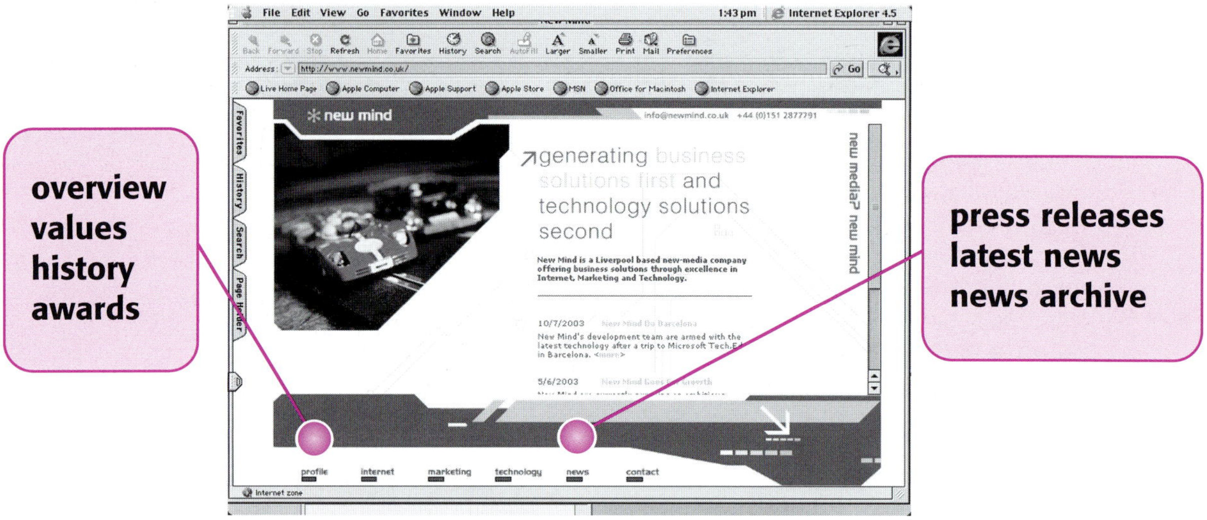

Getting started

Always check with a teacher first and get their permission before using the Internet. They will supervise your work and protect your security.

Use the website address of the business

If you know the website address of a business you just need to type this into your browser where it says 'address'. You will be directed to the company's home page automatically. The address usually will start with http://www followed by the company. So the address of Sony is http://www.sony.com and Virgin is http://www.virgin.com. Note that addresses can change over time.

Use a search engine

If you do not know the website address of a business, you could use a search engine. Google, Yahoo, Alta Vista, Ask Jeeves and Look Smart are examples.

- Type in address of the search engine, eg http://www.google.com or http://uk.yahoo.com. Many pieces of Internet software list these addresses.
- Type in the name of the business you are looking for and click on 'Search'.
- You will be given a list of contacts. One of these will be the company's website.

Practise your skills

Suggest one piece of information that you might find out about marketing, finance, human resources and production from the Internet site of a large public limited company.

What sort of information can be found at a business website?

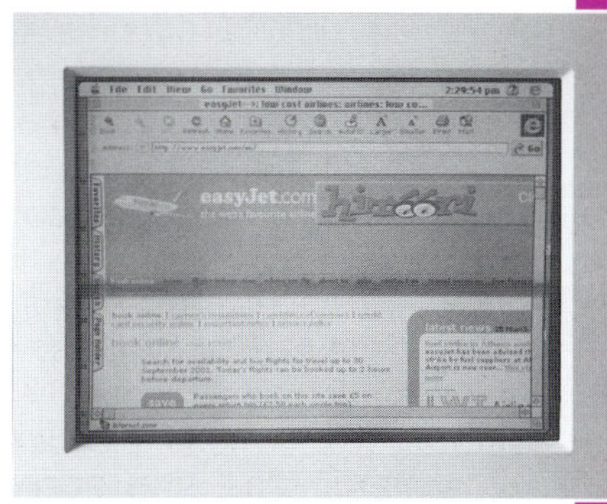

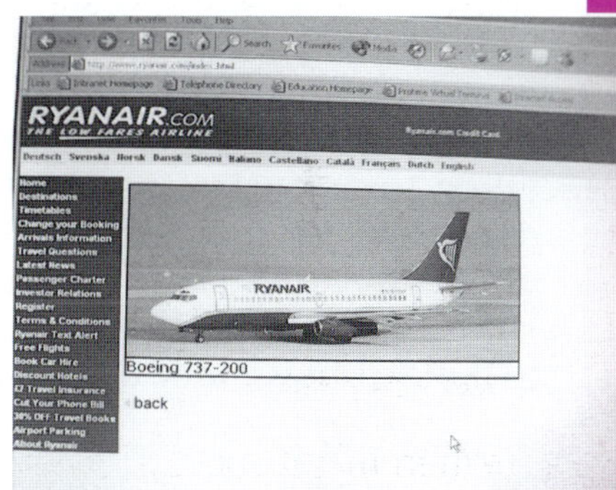

The design of websites will be different for each company. However, the information contained on each site tends to be quite similar. Examples might include:

- the products that the company produces;
- a history of the company;
- objectives of the company and, possibly a mission statement;
- details of key personnel like the chairperson;
- details of its internal organisation;
- information for specific stakeholders like shareholders;
- financial statements such as a profit and loss account and a balance sheet;
- details of the company's commitment to the environment and the community;
- recent news about businesses and press releases.

There are certain advantages and disadvantages of getting information from the Internet.

Advantages

- Information can be gathered from the classroom, the library, from home or anywhere that has Internet access.
- Information can be gathered immediately. There is no waiting time.
- You can print off information so that you have hard copies.
- If you can't find exactly what you are looking for there could be an address, telephone number or email address that you can use to make contact.
- You will have access to information from companies all over the world.

Disadvantages

- Because there is so much information on the Internet it may take time to find exactly what you are looking for.
- Some of the information may not be accurate. Information on the Internet is unregulated. This means that it is not checked by an independent body.
- Many websites on the Internet are rarely updated. Therefore some of the information may be out of date.

Other information

You will be able to find lots of other information from the Internet that will be useful when producing your portfolio.

- Many statistics on business can be found at websites for organisations such as the Office for National Statistics (http://www.ons.gov.uk) and the Department for Trade and Industry (http://www.dti.gov.uk)
- Newspapers, such as the *Financial Times* (http://www.ft.com), and *The Guardian* (http://www.guardian.co.uk) can also be found.
- Production and human resource information can be found on the British Standards Institution site (http://www.bsi.org.uk) and the Investors in People site (http://www.iipuk.co.uk).
- Market research and advertising information can be found from Mintel (http://www.mintel.co.uk) and the Advertising Standards Authority (http://asa.org.uk).

You can use a search engine to find out this information. For example, if you want to find out about contracts of employment, type 'contracts of employment' into a search engine. You will be given many links. Click on the most suitable until you find what you are looking for.

Email

EMAIL allows you to send and receive information electronically. Messages, letters, documents, drawings, photographs, diagrams, numerical data and even moving pictures can be sent using email. Most commonly it is used to send messages. It is a powerful means of communication. This is because information can be sent anywhere in the world almost instantly. All you need to use email is access to a computer and an email address. **Always check with a teacher first before using email. They will supervise your work and advise you on the steps that must be taken to protect your safety and security. Your teacher should always make the first contact when using email, for example making contact with a business.**

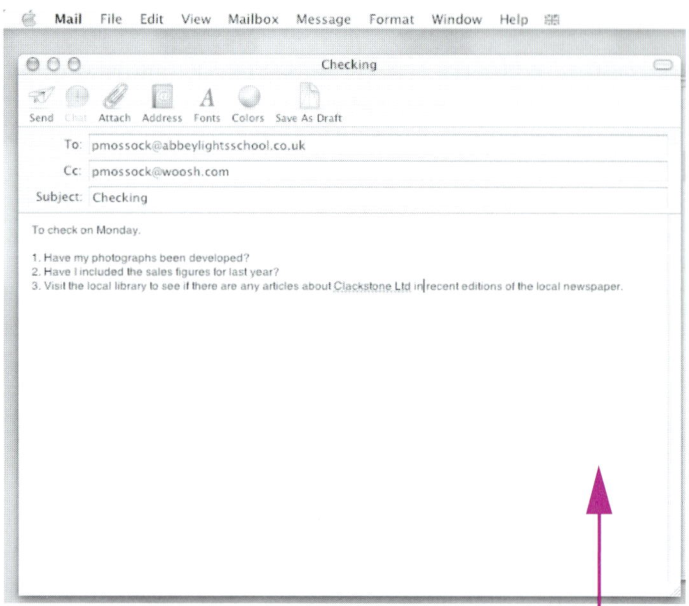

When might you use email for your work?

- Asking for specific information from a business.
- Receiving and downloading information from a business.
- Sending work that you have done to your teacher for checking or marking.
- Sending work that you have done at home to school, where it can be printed off.

There are certain advantages and disadvantages of using email.

Advantages

- Messages and information can be sent instantly, there is no time delay.
- All messages can be stored, so records can be kept.
- It is cheap. For example, a 500 page document could be sent from the UK to Australia for a few pence. If sent by post it might cost several pounds.
- Because it is fast, many messages per day can be exchanged with the same person. It's almost like having a conversation.
- It can be used 24 hours a day and 365 days a year.
- Any type of document or image can be sent.

Disadvantages

- Some business people get lots and lots of emails. Therefore you may have to wait a while for a reply.
- People can ignore emails if they choose. If you need a definite response it may be better to use the telephone. People cannot ignore telephone calls so easily.
- It is sometimes difficult to contact the person you are trying to communicate with. The business might have an email address but an individual in the business might not.

Practise your skills

Write down the steps you would need to take to email a large plc to ask for a copy of its Annual Report and Accounts.

Using attachments

It is possible to send a copy of a computer file with an email message. It is sent as an ATTACHMENT. To do this, click on the attachments tab in your browser mail or email reader and follow the instructions. Different browsers might operate slightly differently.

Attachments are useful when sending large amounts of information or information that is already stored on computer. For example, a business might reply to your email by saying that it has sent a copy of a report you were interested in as an attachment.

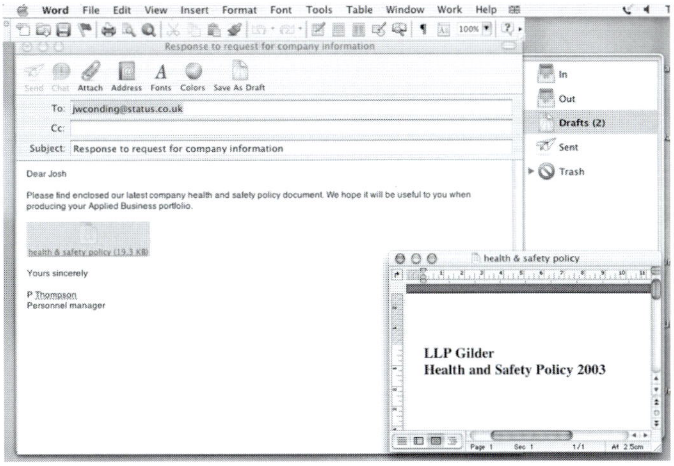

Tips on using the Internet and email

- **Always check with a teacher for their approval before using the Internet or email. They will supervise your work and advise you about how to protect your safety and security when using the Internet or email.**
- Know what information you are aiming to find before starting to browse the Internet. It is very easy to get distracted.
- When searching, be very specific when typing in words or terms in the search engine. Otherwise you will get far too many sites.
- If you find a useful website, store it using your favourites or bookmarkers option. You will be able to go back to it more easily.
- If a website is slow or unavailable, try again later.
- Only use official business websites.

key terms

Attachments - *copies of computer documents or images files that are sent with an email.*
Email - *a means of sending and receiving messages and information electronically.*

key terms key terms key terms key terms key terms key terms ke

portfolio practice

You want to find businesses in the local area to investigate. You would like to work in school and at home on your portfolio and to get help from friends and relatives. Suggest how you might make use of:

- an Internet search engine;
- email;
- an attachment.

6 Using company Annual Reports and Accounts

What is an Annual Report and Accounts?

Every year limited companies produce an important document called the ANNUAL REPORT AND ACCOUNTS. They have to do this by law. The Annual Report and Accounts must then be sent to the Registrar of Companies at Companies House. It can be viewed by anyone there. The document is produced to give shareholders information about the performance and progress of the company. However, it may be used by other stakeholders and members of the public.

The shares of public limited companies are sold openly on stock exchanges. Private limited companies tend to sell shares to family and friends. So you might find it easier to obtain the Annual Report and Accounts of plcs, which are often presented in glossy and colourful booklets.

How can you get an Annual Report and Accounts?

Annual Reports and Accounts might be obtained from the following sources. **You must always check with your teacher first before making contacts to protect your security.**

- Visit company websites on the Internet. Some might include their Annual Reports and Accounts or financial information from the accounts, such as sales or costs.
- Write or email a company that you are interested in through your teacher. They might be prepared to send you a copy. Explain that you are a student doing some research for your GCSE Applied Business portfolio.
- Your teacher, school library or local library might have copies.
- The *Financial Times* Annual Reports Service can supply the Annual Reports and Accounts of plcs. A number is given to telephone each day in the newspaper. Or you can visit their website at http://ft.ar.wilink.com to order copies.

Practise your skills

Obtain the Annual Reports and Accounts of two companies in different industries. Identify four differences in their presentation.

What useful information do Annual Reports and Accounts contain?

Much of the information in Annual Reports and Accounts is needed by law. Not all of it will be useful to you and some of it is detailed and technical. Some, though, will be very important in helping you to produce your portfolio.

Chairman's statement

One of the Chairman's jobs is to tell shareholders how well the company is doing. A statement is written every year in the Annual Reports and Accounts. The statement tells the reader how well the company has performed and what plans it has for the future. The chairman comments on things such as turnover, profit, dividends, growth, new products and investments. Below are extracts from the statements of various Annual Reports and Accounts.

'Overall the group opened 120 new stores, a record level which says much about the success of our retail brands and the confidence we have in future growth. Many of the stores have innovative new formats, including the Comet Destination and Big QW stores in the UK.'

Source: adapted from Chairman's Statement, Kingfisher plc which owns retails stores such as Comet, Woolworth's and Superdrug, *Annual Report and Accounts* 2000.

'Given our confidence in the future growth of our business, the Board is proposing a final dividend of 0.7 pence a share, which increases the total dividend ... to 1.4 pence per share.'

Source: adapted from Chairman's Statement, MFI Furniture Group PLC, *Annual Report and Accounts* 2000.

'I am pleased to announce pre-tax profits for the year to 27 May 2000 have increased by 13% to £23m. This solid performance has been achieved on a 17% increase in turnover...'

Source: adapted from Chairman's Statement, Monsoon the clothes retailer, *Annual Report and Accounts* 2000.

Chief executive's review or operating review

The chief executive is the senior manager and is involved in the day to day running of the business. This review has information about the company's trading activities during the year. It can be more detailed than the chairperson's statement and could be quite helpful to you. It may include information about:

- the operations of the business:
- the trading activities of each division of the business;
- new products and markets that the company is looking into;
- company employees;
- changes to the structure of the company;
- future objectives and changes such as new investments.

Practise your skills

Look at the Chairman's Statements above. What has happened to the businesses?

Profit and loss account

The Annual Report and Accounts contain a statement showing the profit and loss account of a business. The profit and loss account can be used to see how well the company has performed. The main figures that you might be most interested in are turnover, costs and profit. The profit and loss account for Beazer Group Plc, the housebuilders, is shown below. Note that this year's and last year's figures are shown. This allows comparisons to be made.

Beazer Group Plc
Group profit and loss account
Year to 30 June 2000

	2000 £m	1999 £m
Turnover	**840.6**	701.7
Cost of sales	**(696.7)**	(575.1)
Gross Profit	**143.9**	126.6
Administration expenses	**(39.9)**	(34.9)
Operating Profit	**104.0**	91.7
Net interest payable	**(9.6)**	(10.1)
Profit On Ordinary Activities Before Taxation	**94.4**	81.6
Taxation on profit on ordinary activities	**(25.5)**	(22.0)
Profit On Ordinary Activities After Taxation	**68.9**	59.6
Dividends	**(24.6)**	(22.5)
Retained Profit For The Year	**44.3**	37.1

Turnover is money earned from sales. Turnover has risen over the year.

Cost of sales are the costs directly related to building the houses. These costs have risen.

Operating profit is turnover minus costs of sales and expenses. Turnover has risen more than costs and expenses so operating profit has increased.

Profit after taxation and interest has been paid has risen.

After dividends have been paid to shareholders, the profit left is retained in the company. This has risen.

Source: adapted from Beazer Group Plc, *Annual Report and Accounts*, 2000.

Balance sheet

Another important financial statement contained in the Annual Report and Accounts is the balance sheet. This gives information about the company's assets, liabilities and capital. Some of the terms in the balance sheet might be unfamiliar because balance sheets often include different items. But they will all show some figures for fixed assets, current assets, current liabilities, net assets and shareholders funds. The balance sheet for Silentnight Holdings Plc, the domestic furniture group, is shown here.

Source: adapted from Silentnight Holding Plc, *Annual Report and Accounts*, 2000.

Silentnight Holdings Plc
Balance Sheet
as at 27 January 2000

	2000 £'000	1999 £'000
Fixed assets		
Intangible assets	**-**	1,932
Tangible assets	**43,057**	54,240
Investments	**4,076**	4,028
	47,133	60,200
Current assets		
Stocks	**10,974**	13,913
Debtors	**28,945**	33,177
Cash at bank and in hand	**46,334**	12,666
	86,253	59,756
Creditors: amounts falling due within one year	**43,223**	44,832
Net current assets	**43,030**	14,924
Total assets less current liabilities	**90,163**	75,124
Creditors: amounts falling due after more than one year	**2,789**	13,562
Provision for liabilities and charges	**180**	185
	2,969	13,747
Net assets	**87,194**	61,377
Capital and reserves		
Called up share capital	**4,685**	4,685
Share premium account	**1,084**	1,084
Revaluation reserve	**4,767**	4,911
Profit and loss account	**76,658**	50,697
Equity shareholders' funds	**87,194**	61,377

The fixed assets of the business such as shops and equipment have fallen.

Current assets have risen.

Money that has to be paid back in the short term has fallen.

Working capital (current assets-current liabilities) has increased.

Net assets have risen.

Practise your skills

(a) Look at the profit and loss account of Beazer Group Plc. Calculate the percentage change in (i) turnover, (ii) cost of sales, (iii) expenses and (iv) profit after taxation.

(b) Look at the balance sheet for Silentnight Holdings Plc. What is the value of (i) working capital (net current assets) and (ii) shareholders' funds in both years?

Other information

- Social accounts. The Annual report and Accounts is used to comment on the commitment of the business to stakeholders other than shareholders, for example, the environment, their employees and the local community. This is called SOCIAL ACCOUNTING.
- Annual Reports and Accounts will often contain graphs, charts, tables, diagrams, maps and photographs that you might use when preparing materials for your portfolio. The map and graphs here are from a Matalan Annual Report and Accounts. Matalan is a national retailer of clothes.
- At the back of most reports is a table that shows key financial information over a five year period. This might be helpful when making comparisons or looking at trends taking place. For example, you might be able to draw a graph showing how turnover has changed over a five year period.

Source: adapted from Matalan, *Annual Report and Accounts*.

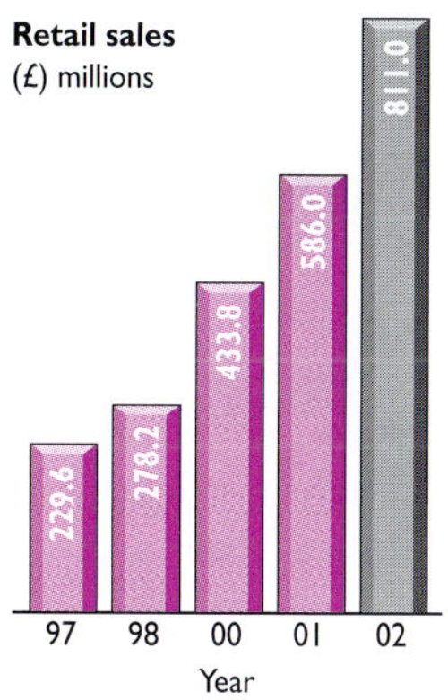

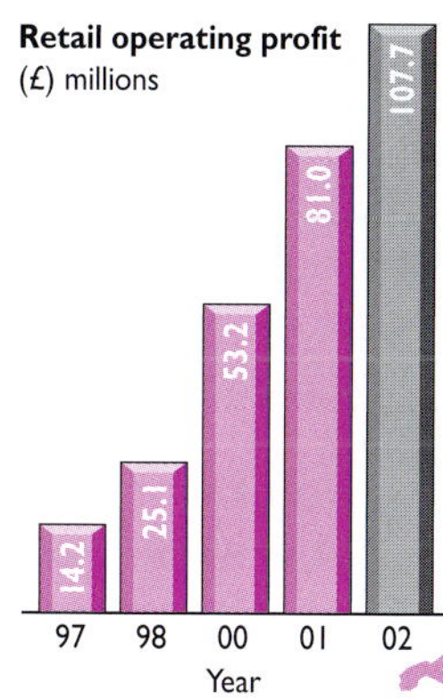

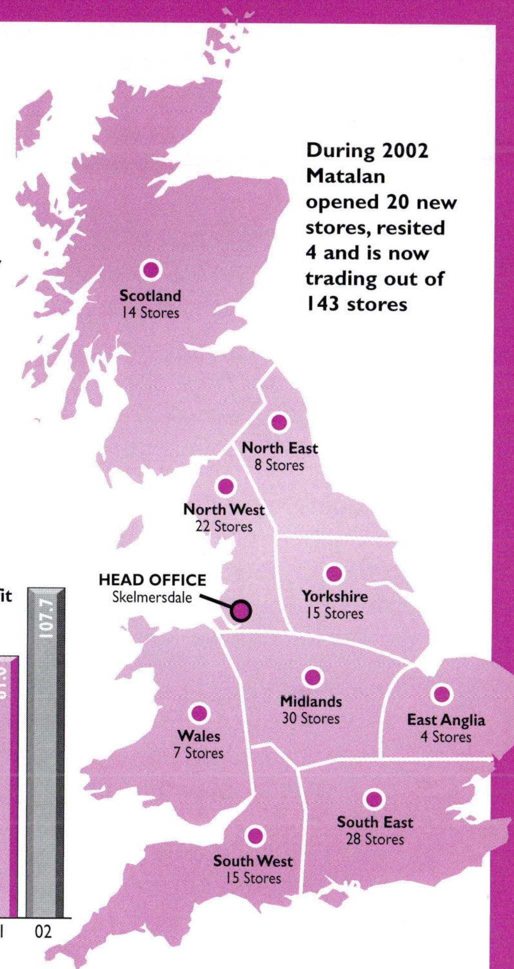

Tips on using Annual Reports and Accounts

- There will be some terms in the profit and loss account and balance sheet that you might not understand. Don't let this stop you from using them. Get help from your teacher with difficult language.
- More information can be found about the figures in the profit and loss account and balance sheet in the NOTES TO THE ACCOUNTS.
- Annual Reports and Accounts are written mainly for shareholders. They tend to focus on good news and say a lot less about bad news.

key terms

Annual Report and Accounts - *a booklet produced by limited companies every year to inform shareholders about performance and progress.*
Social accounting - *reporting on how a business affects society as a whole.*
Notes to the accounts - *further information about figures in the accounts.*

key terms key terms key terms key terms key terms key terms ke

portfolio practice

What does the information above about Matalan show? Write a 100-150 word report.

7 Using newspapers, magazines and reference material

How can you use publications?

Your school library, local library or your Business Studies department will probably have a wide selection of newspapers, magazines and reference books. These will be a good source of information for your portfolio. They will provide written information, photographs, diagrams, tables, graphs and charts.

You should be careful not to copy information directly from newspapers, books and magazines. You must read and use them as source material and then use your own words to show your ideas and thoughts. The following steps might help you to do this.

- Read the article once all the way through.
- Read it again highlighting key words or phrases.
- Make a list of the key words and phrases.
- Use your list to write your own account. Do not look at the article again unless you really have to.
- You should credit the original source of your ideas. **Always check with your teacher first, who will be able to tell you what material you can use and how you can use it.**

Tips on using newspapers, magazines and reference material

- Take photocopies of articles from newspapers, magazines and reference books. This allows you to work outside the library or classroom. It will also save you carrying bulky resources around with you. You should use a filing system to store them.
- It is easy to waste time when 'flicking through' written information. Books have an index and most magazines have a contents page. To avoid wasting time make sure that you know exactly what you are looking for.
- Don't ignore sources because you think the language is difficult. Some articles may look difficult, but you can always get help from your teacher with language.
- If you do not know exactly what you are looking for, using a CD Rom of newspapers or the Internet will save you lots of time and remove the frustration when searching.

Practise your skills

In each case state whether you would use a newspaper, magazine or reference book to find the following information.

1. *The meaning of the term 'stakeholders'.*
2. *Details of the chancellor's budget.*
3. *The amount of profit made by a plc.*
4. *Examples of types of advertising.*
5. *Factors that influence the location of businesses.*

Newspapers

The main advantage of using newspapers is that the information will be up to date. Many newspapers are published every day. Some are available over the Internet.

National daily newspapers

Daily newspapers include large 'broadsheet' papers such as *The Guardian*, *The Independent*, *The Daily Telegraph* and *The Times*, and also 'tabloid' papers such as *The Daily Mail* and *The Daily Mirror*. Some newspapers have a special business section, sometimes a few pages long. These sections contain:

- reports, such as details of the main competitors in an industry;
- special features, such as the development of small businesses;
- interviews with business people, such as the Chairperson of a plc;
- business statistics, such as share prices;
- economic data, such as unemployment, interest, exchange and inflation rates.

The *Financial Times* is a specialist newspaper devoted almost entirely to business and finance. It is divided into two main sections.

- One section contains listings of prices such as shares, bonds, investment funds, foreign currencies and commodities.
- The other section contains up to date business news reports, features and case studies.

Sunday newspapers

Sunday newspapers, such as *The Sunday Times* and *The Observer*, also have special business sections. There are sometimes 'pull outs' or 'mini-newspapers' which are included with the main newspaper. The *Sunday Business* is a specialist business newspaper.

Local newspapers

Local newspapers might also be useful. They might provide background information on local business or give ideas for local businesses to investigate.

Practise your skills

In what type of newspaper are you most likely to find the following information?

- *Information on the performance of the car industry in the year 2000.*
- *The share price of a plc yesterday.*
- *A builder, who is a sole trader, has just announced his business is growing.*

Magazines

Numerous magazines are published that might contain useful information. They might be in your local or school library or your teacher might have some back issues. Local business people or family members might also have copies. Some magazines are also available over the Internet.

Business related magazines

There are many different business related magazines. *EN*, for example, contains case studies of business people. *Management Today* is a magazine aimed at business people and those with an interest in business. It contains articles about businesses, business people, management and new developments in the world of business.

Economics related magazines

These are magazines that often include information about external conditions that affect businesses, such as inflation, the exchange rate and interest rates. *The Economist*, for example, has such articles.

Government publications

The government publishes a number of books such as *Economic Trends*, the *Annual Abstract of Statistics* and *Labour Market Trends*. They contain statistics about industry, business and the economy. The government also publishes reports which might be useful, for example about the amount of pollution in the UK.

Trade magazines

Many magazines are produced that are aimed at particular businesses or business operations. They contain information specific to a particular area of business, for example *Accounting Today* (Accounting), *Marketing Today* (Marketing), *People Management* and *Labour Research* (Human resources), or occupations such as *Caterer and hotelkeeper* or *The Grocer*.

Local magazines

Examples include publications by local learning and skills councils or organisations aiming to help business get government and EU grants to locate in an area.

Company magazines

Some businesses produce magazines for their employees which contain a variety of useful information. For example, *Ford News*, produced by the motor car manufacturer Ford, contains information about employees, changes to the business and new products.

Practise your skills

A national business is moving its factory to another area. It will have to finance this move by borrowing or obtaining other funds. It wants to find out about the funds available and other businesses' experience, and explain how the changes will affect its employees. Explain how information in magazines might be useful to this business.

Reference books

Business Studies reference books and textbooks may be one of your main sources of information. You might use to books to find out:

- how businesses organise themselves;
- about the law is designed to protect workers;
- the methods of communication businesses might use;
- the external factors that might affect businesses;
- the factors that affect business location.

Your school or local library and your Business Studies department will have books that you can use. You may even be issued with a book for this course. Examples of reference books that might be useful are:

- main textbooks - these will be particularly useful when learning about business theory;
- a dictionary of business terms or an English dictionary which might help you with difficult language in articles or Business Studies terms;
- local trade directories or *Yellow Pages* - these are useful for finding businesses in the local area and their telephone numbers.

CD Roms

Some newspapers are available on CD Rom. If your school or local library has them they are very helpful. A CD Rom might contain every copy of a particular newspaper for a whole year. There is also a search facility that can help you find specific information. For example, you may wish to gather information about a company such as Vodafone. All you need to do is type Vodafone into the computer. This gives you a list that contains every article in the newspaper that mentions Vodafone. You can search through the list to find the information that you want.

Other material

There is a variety of other written and visual material that you might use to gather information for your portfolio.

- Business price lists, brochures and catalogues. These will give you information about the products that a business produces and the prices. They can be used to look at how businesses compete with each other and to compare prices.
- Publicity leaflets and advertisements. These will help you to show the main promotional methods used by businesses.
- Reports and market research findings. Organisations such as Mintel or Gallup publish reports and articles on marketing and market research findings.

portfolio practice

Read the article below. Using the steps listed on page 28, write your own summary in three sentences.

Pace Micro tunes to exports

PACE MICRO TECHNOLOGY, the maker of set top boxes, plans to strengthen its position in overseas markets to offset the fall in profits in the UK. Last year the company cut 200 staff and yesterday it announced a fall in its share price by 5.75p (a 10% fall) to 50p. The company is confident that supply contracts in Europe, Asia and the US will rejuvenate the business following a poor 2002. A deluge of new entrants in the free-to-view market and a fall in prices was blamed for the £185.2 million slump in turnover to the year ended May 31 2003. Set top sales volumes fell 41% to 1.3 million. Neil Graydon, President of Pace's American arm, said 'We see the UK as still being dominant, but with increased competition, demand is not going to be at the same level'. Pace hopes that overseas sales will increase by 20% by the end of the year. It hopes by the end of the financial year that new deals overseas will move the business towards break-even.

Source: adapted from *The Guardian*, 18.7.2003.

8 Visiting business organisations

Why visit a business?

A

Visiting a business is an ideal way to find out information. A visit to a business is interesting, exciting and a chance to get all your questions answered. You can also see the business in action and get a real appreciation of its daily operations.

When producing your portfolio you have to choose two businesses for Unit 1 and one business for Unit 2. It may be a good idea to choose at least one business for each unit to visit.

The photographs here show different types of business that you might visit. Looking at the photographs you can see some information that you might be able to find out.

- Photograph A shows a small business that makes pottery. It shows the materials that are being used.
- Photograph B shows a production line in a large motor car factory. It shows the machinery that is being used.
- Photograph C shows a call centre. It shows the jobs the staff are doing, answering the telephone and dealing with customer enquiries.
- Photograph D shows how customers are served at a retailer.

B

If you were to visit these businesses you might find out a lot more. For example, you might:

- be able to appreciate the working conditions;
- find out about the rights of the workers;
- get the opportunity to talk to staff and ask questions.

C

D

Practise your skills

You are visiting the businesses in the photographs. List three different things that you might want to find out about each business.

Choosing a business to visit

Class visits to businesses will be arranged by your teacher. They will make sure that all school regulations and laws regarding visits are met. You can discuss with your teacher the type of business you could visit to help produce your portfolio. Some businesses might be more suitable to visit than others. You might think about the following when making a decision about which business to visit.

Visits

Is someone prepared to talk to you?
It will be helpful if there is a contact who is prepared to talk to your class, answer questions or arrange interviews. Sometimes a personnel officer might be prepared to do this. Or the owner of a small business might be flexible enough to take time out of the working day to show students around.

Contacts
Your teacher may have built up contacts in the area with businesses that will allow a visit and will give information.

Transport
You might have to choose a business which is within a short travelling distance. You teacher is unlikely to organise a visit to a farm in Cumbria if your school is in Cornwall.

Safety
It might not be possible to visit certain parts of a business for safety reasons, such as the actual part of a factory that manufactures products. This might affect your portfolio unless there are other ways of getting this information, for example from brochures, videos or an explanation from a manager.

Timing
It is important that the visit fits in with when you have to produce your portfolio. If a business is only prepared to let a class visit after the portfolio must be handed in, then another business might have to be chosen.

Ease of access, space and organisation
A business would need to be large enough to take a group of students or be able to organise a visit so that many students can visit different people.

Availability of information
Some businesses will be able to give lots of information. Others will not. For example, many business in the pharmaceuticals industry have products protected by patents, which prevents other businesses bringing out similar products. They might not be willing to give details of production methods. Some businesses might not want to give out information about their sales turnover in case rivals find out.

Business policy
Some businesses do not allow school visits. This might be the policy of the company or the decision of the owner. It is often useful to consider a number of businesses in case it is not possible to visit the one in which you are most interested.

Knowledge
It is sometimes useful to chose a business that you know something about. This might be a large well known business, a business where a relative works or a business that has received students before.

Practise your skills

Write down two reasons why you might want to visit:
- *a local CD and DVD shop as part of your Unit 1 portfolio;*
- *a franchise as part of your Unit 1 portfolio;*
- *a well known international company as part of your Unit 1 portfolio;*
- *a car manufacturer in Kent for Unit 2 of your portfolio if you were a student in Maidstone.*

Preparing for a visit

Once your visit has been set up you need to begin your preparation. If you are prepared you will get more out of your visit. Even if the visit has been organised by your teacher you should still prepare thoroughly. What should you do?

Establish purpose

You need to know exactly what you want to find out. Your teacher should explain to your contact in the business what you would like to see. For example, if you were visiting a cement works to find out how the product is made you might want to look at production facilities.

Do some research

It helps if you know a little bit about the business before you go. If you already know something about its history, products and organisation you will get more out of the visit. This knowledge will also help you get on well with your contact. Therefore, do a little research before you go.

Write some questions

During the visit you will want to ask questions. Have them ready before you go. You could write out a list, but you might prefer to use a questionnaire. A questionnaire will be useful if you interview staff.

Take appropriate equipment

You must decide how to record answers. You might have to make notes, so take a notepad and pencil. If the business has given permission for you to take photographs or a video, take a camera that is easy to use.

Dress appropriately

You should dress smartly when visiting a business. You are representing your school and yourself. You need to make a good impression. If you are asked to wear a particular item of clothing, such as strong shoes, make sure you do.

Practise your skills

Write a list of 10 questions that you might ask if you were going to visit a bank to find out about its customer services.

The DOs and DON'Ts during the visit

DOs

- ✔ Be prompt for your visit. Perhaps arrive a few minutes early.
- ✔ Follow all instructions given to you by your contact. Some business premises are dangerous and you will need to follow special health and safety procedures. For example, you may be asked to wear earplugs or protective clothing.
- ✔ Be courteous at all times.
- ✔ Show an interest in what is going on and what you are being told.
- ✔ Make brief notes while you are there and write them up as soon as you get back.

DON'Ts

- ✘ Do not talk to staff while they are working unless you have permission or you are invited to do so.
- ✘ Do not be afraid to ask 'spur of the moment' questions.
- ✘ Do not wander off on your own while on business premises, unless you are invited to do so.
- ✘ Do not take photographs or videos unless you have permission. Some businesses do not allow photographs of their operations to be taken.

Further benefits of business visits

Some of the main benefits of visiting a business have been explained. However, there are others that you might consider.

- The information that you gather is likely to be original. You will get more credit for using original information when your portfolio is assessed. It will also be up to date information.
- You may be able to collect internal documents used by businesses. For example, you might get copies of application forms that they use. However, get permission before taking them away.
- If your visit is a success you might get the chance to build links with the business. This means you may be able to gather more information.
- With permission, you may be able to take photographs, film activities with a video camera and tape record interviews with staff.

portfolio practice

Your teacher has organised a visit to a local manufacturer.
(a) What research might you do before going?
(b) Suggest two things that you might want to find out about its:

- marketing;
- finance;
- communications;
- production.

9 Using work experience

What is work experience?

Visiting a business is a good way of obtaining original information for your portfolio. However, you can also make the most of any work experience that has been arranged by your school. If you are placed in a business you will be on the premises for a long period of time. This will allow you to look carefully at various business departments and gather a lot of useful information. Some examples are shown below.

Watching a production worker

Helping to design an advertisement for the marketing department

Sitting in on a finance meeting

There are different types of work experience that you could be involved in.

- A real work experience in a part-time job that you have.
- A work experience placement organised by your school or college, usually for one or two weeks in school time. This may be compulsory.
- A work experience placement that you have organised on your own, perhaps using a contact like your parents, a friend or a relative. This could be at weekends or in the school holidays.

Practise your skills

What might be the advantages for the students doing the work experience in the situations above?

Induction

Many businesses provide an INDUCTION programme for new staff. The purpose of this is to welcome them, make them feel comfortable and give them information about the business. You will be given a 'mini-induction programme' on your work experience placement. Induction programmes tend to give out general information about the business. In your induction you may be told about:

- the organisation, its history, development, management and activities;
- physical facilities such as toilets and canteen;
- the role and work of supervisors;
- details of your daily activities;
- rules and company regulations;
- health and safety, perhaps shown on a video.

How can you use work experience?

During your placement you may get the chance to see all the different departments in the business. You can watch people doing their jobs and spend time talking to employees. The opportunity for gathering information will be huge. Some of the things you can do are as follows.

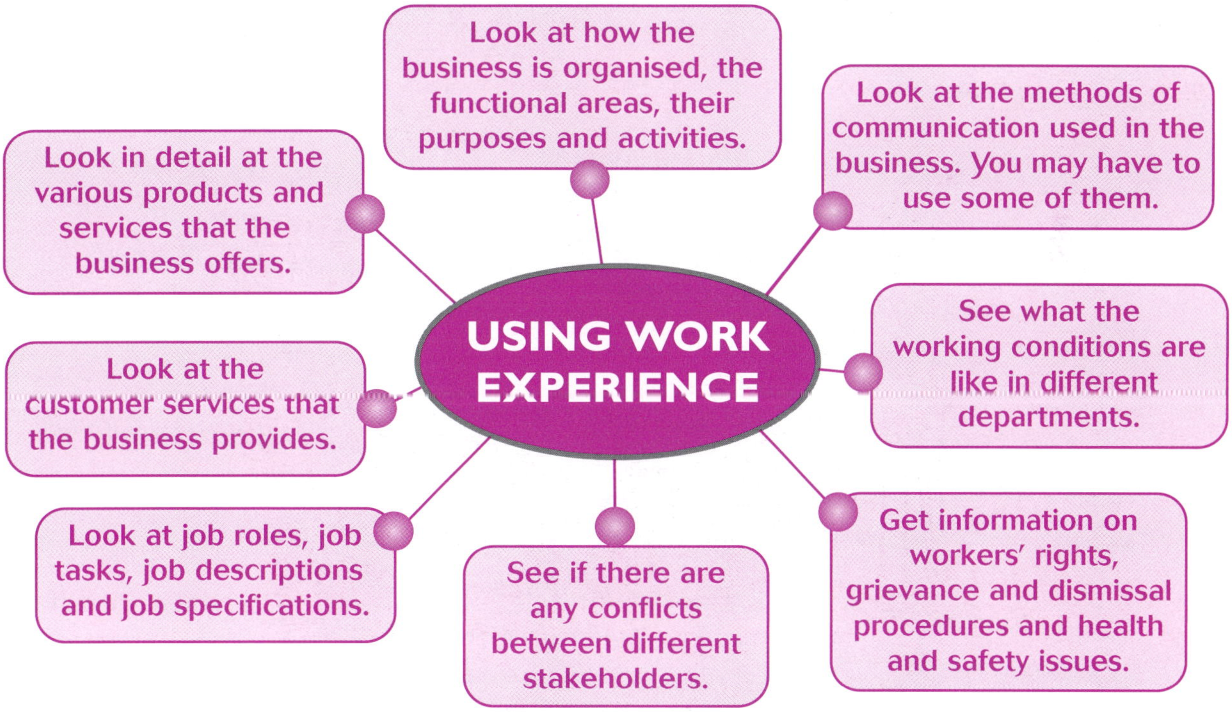

Practise your skills

Which departments might provide information on:
(a) products and customer services;
(b) health and safety issues;
(c) company performance;
(d) manufacturing techniques?

Gathering information

Once you have started your work experience placement you will be able to gather information from a variety of sources. These may include the following.

- Documents given to you during induction.
- Documents that you collect from the various departments during your stay.
- Interviews and conversations with staff and customers.
- Details of personal observations.

You need to keep a record of the information that you gather. Keeping or photocopying any documents that you are given will be a good way. Questionnaires can be used to record information from staff. However, you will need to keep a record of conversations and your personal observations. One way of doing this is to keep a diary of your work experience. Jushna Kuper did a two week placement at a bank. An extract from the first day of her diary is shown below.

Work experience diary

Monday October 13

9.00 – 10.00
Attended an induction session. Saw a video about the history and development of the bank. Met Sue King, my supervisor. She is assistant branch manager. A lot of information about the organisation and security was given. Sue introduced me personally to everyone.

10.00 – 13.00
Spent the rest of the morning with Debbie Price. I helped type some information into the computer. She told me that she enjoyed working there because she got lots of training. She was trained to sell insurance policies to existing customers. She went on a 5 day training course in Birmingham. We had a 10 minute coffee break at 11.15.

13.00 – 14.00
Spent the lunch hour in a staff room with Debbie and two lads. They also said they liked working for the bank. I asked them if it was ever boring and they said no not really.

14.00 – 16.30
Spent all afternoon on the customer services desk. This was really interesting. I watched Suzi and Ng deal with customer queries. I was surprised at how good they were given that they were really young. They said they had been trained well. Towards the end they let me deal with a customer. It was a bit scary and I needed Ng's help. A lady had lost her cheque book. There was a manual to look up procedures for every type of query. I might try and get a photocopy of this later.

Practise your skills

(a) State three things in Jushna's diary above that could be useful for her portfolio.
(b) What should Jushna do before taking a photocopy of the manual?

Preparation for a work experience placement

You need to prepare for your work experience placement in the same way that you would for a business visit. However, because you will be there for a lot longer more preparation will be needed. For example, you might design some questionnaires for staff to complete. Since you are likely to visit different departments you might want to find out different things. Therefore, you might need different sets of questions. For example, the questions you ask employees in the marketing department might be different from those asked in the production department.

Tips on using work experience

- Use your work experience placement as one of the businesses for your investigations.
- It is best to update your diary at the end of every day. If you leave it until the end of the placement, you may have forgotten a lot of useful information.
- If possible choose your own placement. You will be better motivated if you are working in a place of your choice.
- Always ask permission if you want to take internal documents away with you.
- Try to develop a list of contacts so that you can get more information in the future.
- If you are unhappy about some aspect of your work experience speak to your supervisor. Alternatively contact your teacher at school.
- Write a letter of thanks after you have completed your work placement.

portfolio practice

Design a questionnaire that could be used to find out about the training employees are given in the production department of an engineering company or the sales department of a retailer. Use both open and closed questions.

You could take into account the following.

- Amount and frequency of training.
- Types of training.
- Benefits to staff of training.
- Benefits to business of training.
- Quality of training.
- Whether training was enjoyable.
- Whether you were allowed to comment on the training given.

key terms

Induction – *the introduction of a new employee to a business.*

key terms key terms key terms key terms key terms key terms ke

10 Running a mini enterprise

What is a mini enterprise?

You may get the chance to take part in a MINI ENTERPRISE. This is where a group of pupils set up and run a small business enterprise in school. The activity will be supervised by a teacher, but you will run the enterprise. You do all the planning, organisation and development of the business. You may have to raise capital, buy resources, set up production, market the products, keep financial records and measure performance.

Take the example of a group of students who were involved in a mini enterprise at school. The mini enterprise provided a high quality car valeting service for staff.

WASH&DRIVE
Mini Enterprise

A high quality car valeting service

WASH & RINSE £3
FULL VALET £5

Contact
Jeff Sidcup
Horsefield School

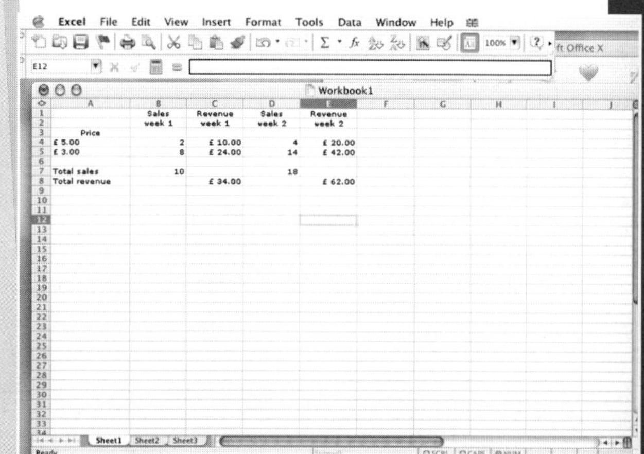

	Sales week 1	Revenue week 1	Sales week 2	Revenue week 2
Price				
£ 5.00	2	£ 10.00	4	£ 20.00
£ 3.00	8	£ 24.00	14	£ 42.00
Total sales	10		18	
Total revenue		£ 34.00		£ 62.00

Practise your skills

What business activities can you identify in the situations above?

How will running a mini enterprise help me with my portfolio? Business theory

When you are running a mini enterprise you will be learning how a business works. Although a mini enterprise is a very small business unit, it will be run along the same lines as a real business.

Consider a group of students who set up a mini enterprise selling soft drinks and confectionery at break and lunch time.

Stakeholders

All businesses have stakeholders. Examples of stakeholders in this mini enterprise will be the owners, the customers, the employees and suppliers. The owners might be students and staff that have bought shares in the enterprise. The customers are likely to be students and staff and employees will be students. Suppliers might be a local cash and carry or a wholesaler. The diagram below shows stakeholders in a school shop.

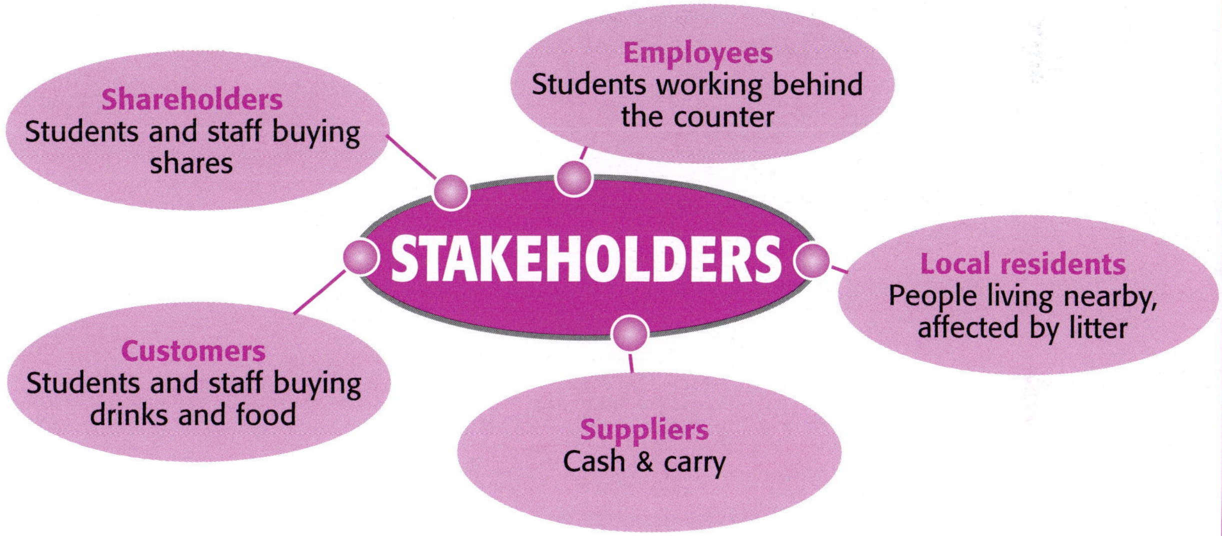

Aims and objectives

The main aim of this mini enterprise might be to make a profit. For example, this enterprise might set monthly profit targets. Another aim might be to expand the business by opening for longer or having more than one sales point in the school.

Finance

This mini enterprise is likely to raise money by selling shares to students and staff. This money will be used to buy stock from suppliers and pay other costs. The company may also have to pay for the use of space in the school to store and sell confectionery.

Operations

Businesses have to obtain, organise and use a variety of resources including people and equipment. This mini enterprise will have to buy stock and resell it. It will need a secure and dry storage area, a counter, a secure container for cash and people to move stock and sell it.

Practise your skills

You have decided to run a mini enterprise that will run a school disco at dinner time. Explain who will be the stakeholders in this enterprise.

Marketing
The mini enterprise might do market research to find out what sort of confectionery customers want. They may also set prices deliberately below those of competitors. Advertising, such as posters around the school, might be used. These are all examples of marketing activities this enterprise might use.

Keeping records
This mini enterprise will be accountable to the shareholders. It will have to keep records of all payments and receipts. It will also have to prepare financial statements to show how well the enterprise has performed, such as the profit and loss account below.

Being involved in a mini enterprise means you will have to understand some business theory to be successful. The knowledge that you develop will help you produce better quality work for your portfolio.

Profit and loss account (£)

Turnover		434
Cost of sales		262
Gross profit		172
Expenses		
Rent	50	
Other costs	60	
		110
Net profit		62

How will running a mini enterprise help me with my portfolio? Skills development

Running a mini enterprise will help you to develop some important skills.

Decision making
Running a mini enterprise will involve making decisions such as:
- what products to supply;
- how finance will be raised to buy resources;
- how the enterprise will be organised, eg who will do what;
- what the enterprise will be called;
- what resources will be needed.

Problem solving
Problems are bound to arise when running a business. You will get the chance to help solve them. For example, you may have to deal with a supplier failing to deliver goods that have been ordered.

Communication
If the flow of information between members of the enterprise is good it will run more smoothly. For example, if your job is to buy stock from suppliers, you will have to communicate with the people in charge of stocks and those who know what customers want.

Practise your skills

Suggest three methods of communication that might be used in a mini enterprise.

Planning
Running a mini enterprise needs a lot of planning. For example, you may be advised to draw up a BUSINESS PLAN. This is a statement that outlines how the enterprise will achieve its aims and objectives. A business plan will give the enterprise a clear idea of its direction and help identify problems before they occur.

Organising
Good organisation will help the enterprise to run smoothly. A leader of the enterprise should be elected. Tasks and responsibilities should be given to all members of the enterprise. If everyone has something specific to do the business will be better run. If deadlines are set in the plan this will also help. Finally, if students work as a team results will be better.

The experience you get using these skills will help you to produce a better portfolio. For example, developing your communication skills will help you deal with gathering information from people in business.

Mini enterprise and Unit 3

When running the mini enterprise you may have to learn about:
- business documents, methods of making and receiving payments and bank accounts;
- costs and break even;
- cash flow forecasting and budgeting;
- profit and loss accounts and balance sheets;
- sources of finance;
- financial planing.

All this, and more, will help you to understand Business Finance in Unit 3 of the Applied Business course.

key terms

Business plan *- a written statement that outlines how a business will achieve its objectives.*
Mini enterprise *– a small business set up and run by students in a school or college.*

key terms key terms key terms key terms key terms key terms ke

portfolio practice

You have joined a mini enterprise group at school and have decided to run a computer design service. You will design and print small items such as birthday cards or party invitations for other people in the school.

(a) State three key decisions that would have to be made.

(b) State two ways in which the enterprise might be marketed.

(c) Why might the enterprise produce a profit and loss account?

11 Graphs, charts, photographs and other visual information

Visual presentation

You should try to present work in your portfolio in a variety of ways. It will make it more interesting. Much of the material in your portfolio will be written. However, there are good reasons for presenting some of it visually.

- It might be easier to understand.
- It can take less time to study and can have a bigger impact on the reader.
- It might be easier to see trends.
- It can be used to make a good impression.
- It can be more concise.

The information here is presented visually in the form of a pie chart, a bar chart, a line graph and a photograph.

Turnover of Sunderland plc
2001

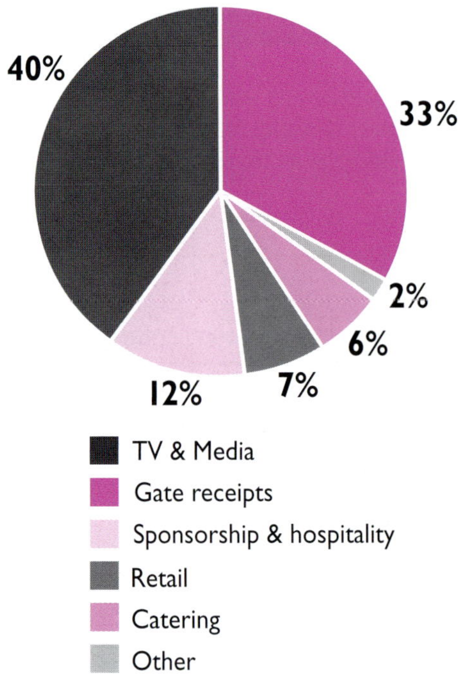

Source: adapted from Sunderland plc, *Annual Report and Accounts*.

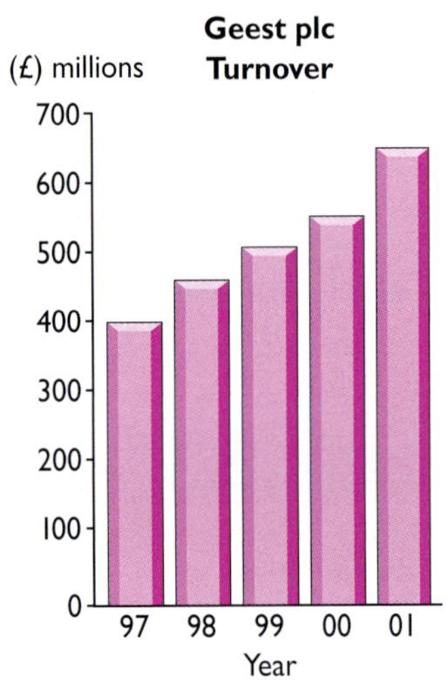

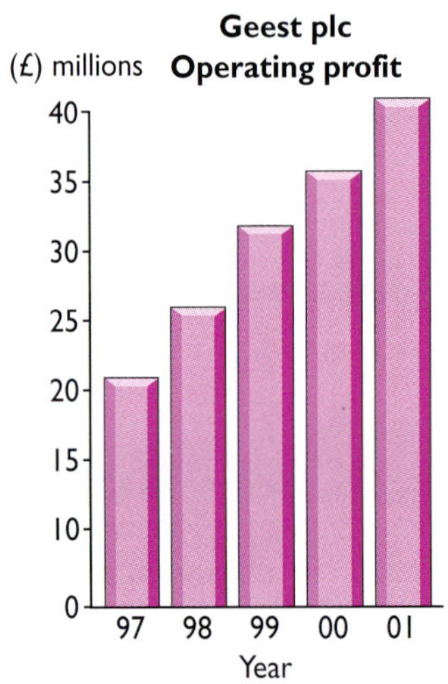

Source: adapted from Geest plc, *Annual Report and Accounts*.

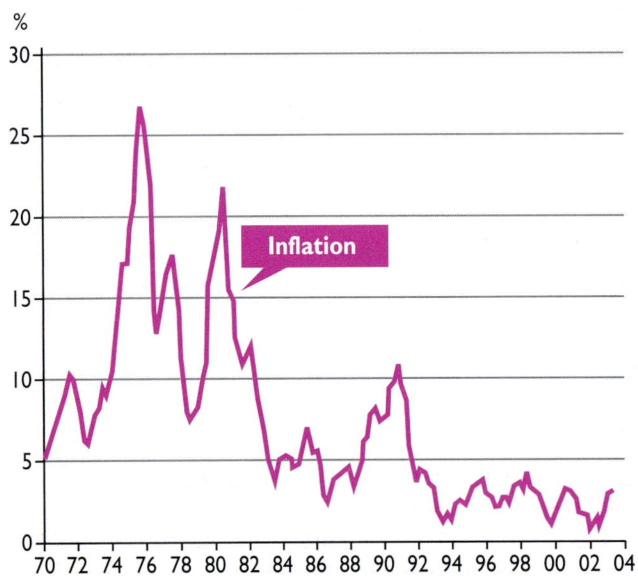

Source: adapted from Datastream.

Practise your skills

What does each of the visual images above show?

Bar charts

A BAR CHART is one of the simplest methods of presenting data. Numerical information is shown by 'bars' or 'blocks'. These can be drawn horizontally or vertically. The longer the bars the more important the DATA. The graph here shows that the number of accidents at Northern Foods has fallen since 1998-99.

Source: adapted from Northern Foods, *Annual Report and Accounts*.

Accident rates: number of reportable accidents per million hours worked

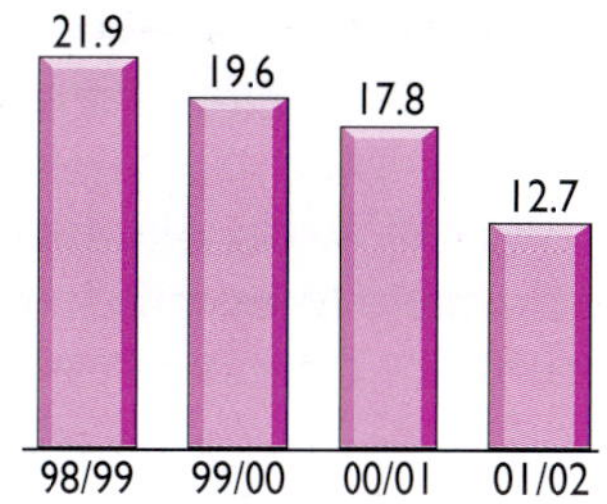

Component bar chart

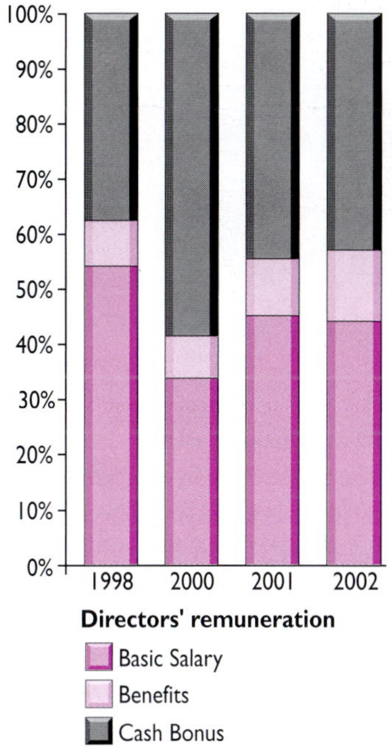

A COMPONENT BAR CHART shows more information. The bars are divided into components or sections. The graph shown is a percentage component bar chart. It shows how the earnings of Matalan directors are split between basic salary, benefits and cash bonuses.

Source: adapted from Matalan, *Annual Report and Accounts*.

Parallel bar chart

A parallel bar chart enables you to show several different sets of data on the same graph. The chart here shows the number of staff employed by Trimwear plc in its different factories over a four year period.

Trimwear, staff employed by location

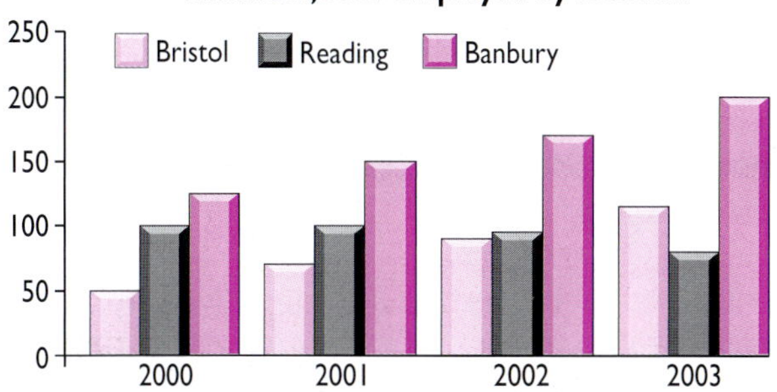

Gain and loss bar chart

A gain and loss bar chart is used to show both positive and negative figures. The chart here shows the profit made by a hair salon. The business was set up in 1998 and after a shaky start profit has risen steadily.

Haircare, profit and loss 1998-2003

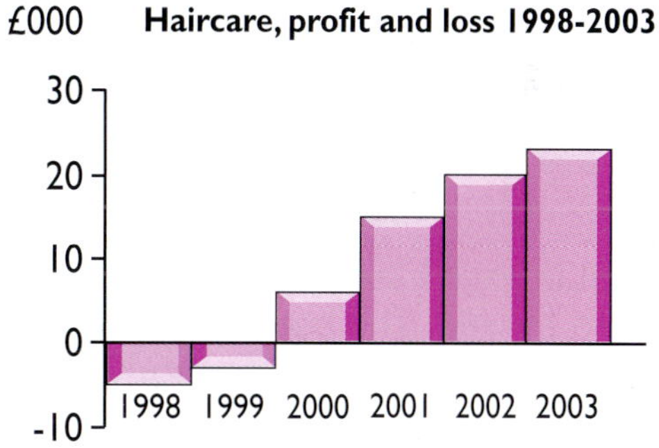

A pictograph or pictogram

A PICTOGRAPH or PICTOGRAM is similar to a bar chart. The difference is that data are represented by symbols. The chart here has been produced by United Utilities. It shows interruptions in the electricity supply per 100 customers.

Interruptions in supply per 100 customers, 1998-2002

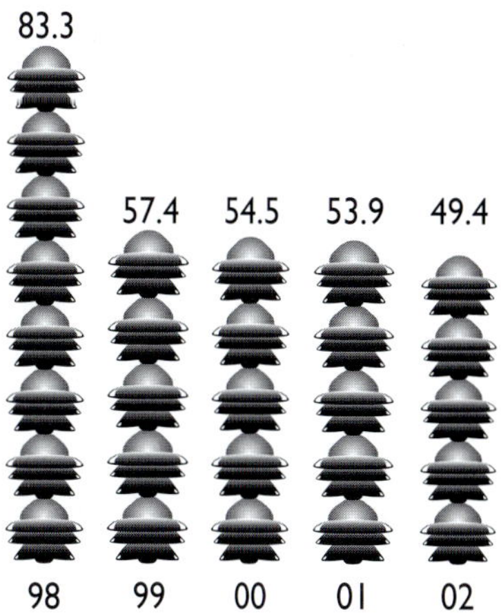

Practise your skills

Draw a simple bar graph to show the data below for Robertsons, a bus company.

Year	1996	1997	1998	1999	2000	2001	2002
Complaints	200	240	290	360	500	310	190

Pie charts

In a PIE CHART all the data are represented by a circle. The circle is divided into segments. Each segment (or piece of pie) represents part of the total data. Some calculations are needed to draw a pie chart. For example, in 2002 AQT Ltd sold 72,000 of its security systems. Of these, 36,000 were sold in the UK, 24,000 in Europe and 12,000 in the US. The 360 degrees in a circle have to be divided between the various segments that make up the circle. In this case there are three segments (UK, Europe and US). The calculations are as follows.

$$\text{UK} = \frac{36{,}000}{72{,}000} \times 360 = 180 \text{ degrees}$$

$$\text{Europe} = \frac{24{,}000}{72{,}000} \times 360 = 120 \text{ degrees}$$

$$\text{US} = \frac{12{,}000}{72{,}000} \times 360 = 60 \text{ degrees}$$

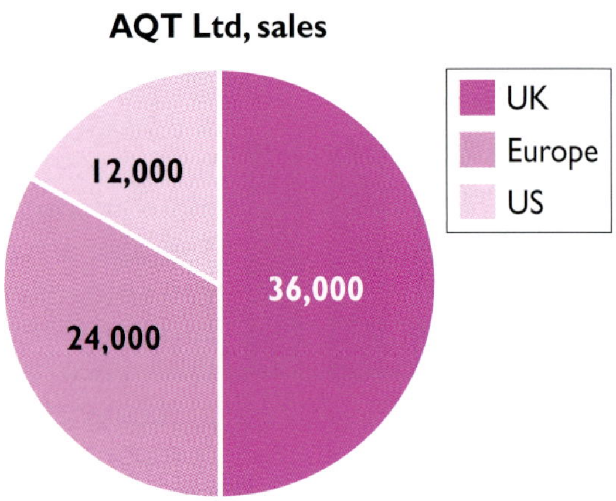

Note that in each case the number sold in each market is divided by the total sold and multiplied by 360. The chart can now be drawn using a protractor. Spreadsheets and drawing programs can also be used to produce pie charts. If the figures for sales in the UK, Europe and the US are placed into a spreadsheet, the program can draw the pie chart from the information.

Line graphs

LINE GRAPHS are common in business. A line graph shows the link between two sets of numerical data. One set of data is shown on the vertical axis and the other on the horizontal axis. The two sets of data must be related in some way. The line graph here shows the share price of Greene King, the brewer, over a two year period. Note that time is always plotted on the horizontal axis in a line graph.

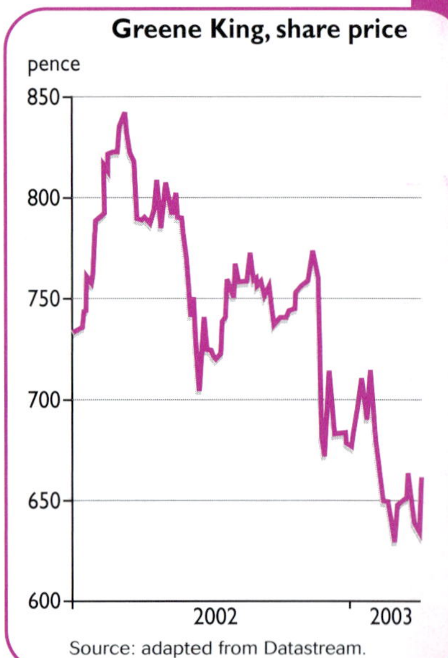

Method	Advantages
Bar graph	Shows data very clearly. Trends and changes can be spotted easily.
Component bar chart	Allows more information to be shown. Allows more comparisons to be made.
Parallel bar chart	Easy to compare changes between components.
Gain and loss bar chart	Shows clearly the difference between positive and negative figures.
Pie chart	Shows immediately the relative importance of different sets of data.
Line graph	Easy to see relationships between two sets of data. Can take measurements from the graph when studying data.

Practise your skills

Look at the line graph for Greene King above. Describe what is happening to its share price in 2002 and 2003.

Photographs

Photographs will make your portfolio more interesting. Also, you may be able to show some information more effectively than describing it in words. For example, you may want to show working conditions or a complicated production process. A photograph may give a much better description than words. Remember it is important to ask permission to take photographs inside businesses.

Other visual images

You may choose to use other visual images. They can be eye catching and can summarise information effectively. Examples include:

- geographical maps, such as maps in an atlas or a local street map;
- mind maps, which can be used to show ideas you have thought up;
- family trees or organisational charts which show links;
- flow diagrams, which show the stages of a process.

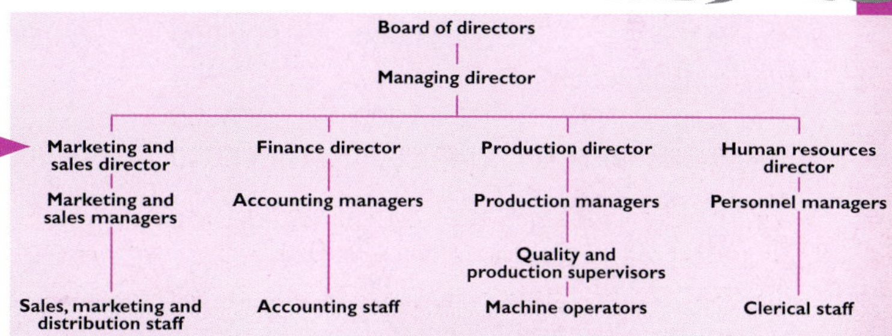

key terms

Bar chart - *a chart where numerical information is represented by bars or blocks.*
Component bar chart – *a chart where each bar is divided into sections to show the components of a total.*
Data – *information.*
Line graph – *a line which shows the link between two sets of numerical data.*
Pictograph or pictogram – *a chart where numerical data are shown by pictorial symbols.*
Pie chart – *a circular chart where segments represent the data.*

portfolio practice

The information below is for Barton Ltd, an insurance broker.

No. of computers in each department

Finance	Human resources	Administration	Sales
12	3	18	39

Hourly wage rates paid to sales staff 1998 - 2003 (£)

1998	1999	2000	2001	2002	2003
4.50	4.60	4.80	4.85	5.00	5.30

(a) Draw a pie chart to show the allocation of computers.
(b) Draw a line graph to show changes in the sales wage rates from 1998 to 2003.

12 Tables, spreadsheets and calculations

What are tables?

You might present some of the information in your portfolio in the form of a table. Tables contain numerical and written information. They are organised into columns (information going down) and rows (information going across). Examples of data shown in tables include:

- financial data, such as the value of sales, costs or salaries of employees;
- numerical data, such as the number of employees or the average number of absences each year;
- other information, such as whether a target has been achieved or not.

An example from the sales department of the Acton Pension Company is shown below. For example, the table shows that the value of sales in the West area of the UK in 2003 were £1.222 million.

Sales department information for the Acton Pension Company, 2003

	UK, North	UK, South	UK, East	UK, West	Rest of Europe	Total
Sales (£)	654,000	870,000	760,000	1,222,000	2,432,00	5,938,000
Sales staff, number	2	4	3	6	8	23
Sales salaries (£)	43,000	99,000	54,000	142,000	210,000	548,000
Other sales costs (£)	112,000	191,000	161,000	212,000	298,000	974,000
Average absence per year, days	4	7	2	3	3	
Target achieved	Yes	No	Yes	Yes	Yes	

Examples of tables found in business include:

- profit and loss accounts, balance sheets, cash flow forecasts and budgets;
- current share prices, highest and lowest prices and how they have changed;
- market research results;
- information about particular industries, such as the output of businesses in the agricultural industry or the number of sole traders and how this has changed over time;
- information about human resources, such as the number of people leaving a business, the number of strikes or the number of people belonging to trade unions.

Analysing tables

Tables might be used in a number of ways. The table here shows the Saturday takings of seven checkout staff in a supermarket. The table might be used:

- to present a mixture of written and numerical data in an organised way. For example, it shows the names of the seven checkout staff and which checkout counter they work at;
- to show the order of importance in data. For example, the table shows that Cheryl is the leader with £54,232. She is 'top of the table'. The data are presented in descending order from the top;
- when it is necessary to perform calculations from the information. In the table here the numerical information is totalled. The takings of each checkout are added to give a total of £337,320.

Employee	Checkout No.	Takings (£)
Cheryl	4	54,232
Tom	6	51,333
Vijay	3	49,876
Karen	1	49,332
Jose Maria	5	46,339
Ken	7	44,332
Jenny	2	41,876
Total		**337,320**

Practise your skills

Look at the table showing data about the Acton Pension Company. Describe:

- *the number of sales staff in each area;*
- *the sales salaries and other sales costs in different areas;*
- *the ability of areas to achieve sales targets.*

Spreadsheets

Some types of data are best presented using a SPREADSHEET. A spreadsheet allows data to be entered, stored and presented in a grid on a computer screen. The grid is made up of a number of 'cells' or blank boxes. These cells are arranged in rows (information across the spreadsheet) and columns (information down the spreadsheet). Each cell may contain information. It will be one of three types.

- **Numerical data** - these are numbers typed into the grid.
- **Text** - these are words typed into the grid. They are often headings.
- **Formulae** - these are instructions that tell the computer what to do with the numbers that have been typed in. For example, the computer might be instructed to add up a column of numbers. Formulae are not shown on a spreadsheet when it is on screen.

The spreadsheet below shows an extract from some customer information for Watsons Ltd, a fruit and vegetable wholesaler. The spreadsheet contains both written and numerical information.

	A	B	C	D	E
1	Customer	Account No.	Credit limit	Total owed	Credit available
2	Smith & Sons	1127	£5000	£3700	£1300
3	Rogers Ltd	1132	£10000	£4100	£5900
4	The Dog & Gun	1143	£5000	£4300	£700
5	Patel	1123	£10000	£7660	£2340
6	Weston Hotel	1162	£15000	£8500	£6500
7	John Carlton	1141	£5000	£0	£5000
8	Wendy Roberts	1161	£5000	£4900	£100
9	Esmee Hall	1135	£5000	£4000	£1000
10	Total		£60000	£37160	£22840

- Column A shows the customer's name.
- Column B shows the customer account number.
- Column C shows how much credit is allowed by Watsons to each customer.
- Column D shows how much each customer currently owes.
- Column E shows how much credit is left to be paid. This is calculated automatically by the program.
- Row 1 shows the column titles.
- Rows 1-9 show the account number, credit limit and credit available for each customer. So cell C6 shows that the Western Hotel had a credit limit of £15,000 and cell E6 shows that it still had £6,500 credit available.
- Row 10 shows the totals. So cell D10 shows the total owed by all business. The totals can be calculated automatically by the spreadsheet as figures are added to the cells.

Data presented in a spreadsheet has certain advantages.

- Numerical data is shown clearly and orderly.
- Numbers in the cells can be added, subtracted, divided and multiplied easily by the program.
- Information in the cells can be changed easily.
- The effect of any changes on other cells is calculated automatically.
- Some programmes allow graphs and charts to be drawn from data on the spreadsheet.

Practise your skills

Look at the spreadsheet above.
(a) How are the figures in column E calculated?
(b) How are the figures in row 10 calculated?

Calculations

When analysing numerical information you may need to do some calculations. This may help you to make comparisons or draw conclusions about the numbers you are looking at.

Proportions

You may want to look at the importance of certain numbers. For example, you may want to compare the amount of money that two businesses spend on research and development (R & D). If Ztex plc spends £9 million and Chemix plc spends £12 million you may decide that Chemix spends the most. However, it might be useful to calculate the proportion of turnover that is spent on R&D. If Ztex has a turnover of £102 million and Chemix £188 million, the proportion each company spends on R & D is:

$$\text{Ztex} = \frac{£9\text{m}}{£102\text{m}} \times 100 = 8.8\%$$

$$\text{Chemix} = \frac{£12\text{m}}{£188\text{m}} \times 100 = 6.4\%$$

You may now decide that Ztex spends more on R&D because its spending is a bigger proportion of turnover. Ztex's 8.8% is bigger than Chemix's 6.4%.

Trends and patterns

One way of identifying trends and patterns is to calculate percentage changes. For example, if profit rises from £120,000 to £150,000, what is the percentage increase? The formula needed to work this out is:

$$\text{Percentage change} = \frac{\text{Difference}}{\text{Original number}} \times 100$$

In this case the difference between the two numbers is £30,000 (£150,000 – £120,000). The original number is the first one, ie £120,000. Therefore the percentage change in this case is:

$$\frac{30{,}000}{£150{,}000} \times 100 = 20\%$$

So profits have fallen by 20%.

Practise your skills

The amount spent on training and the wage bill for each department is shown below for Harrison Ltd, an engineering company.

(£000)

	Human resources	Finance	Production	Administration	Sales
Training	8	12	40	6	10
Wages	60	80	200	120	100

Which department spends the greatest proportion of money on training in relation to its wage bill?

Financial ratios

When looking at the performance and the financial state of a business accountants use FINANCIAL RATIOS. These can be calculated by using figures from the accounts. A ratio may be one number expressed as a percentage of another or one divided by another. The two numbers must be related, like profit and turnover for example. Two useful ratios are the return on capital invested in the business and the profit margin. In 2003 Milford plc made a net profit of £2.5 million. Its turnover was £30 million and the capital invested was £20 million.

$$\text{Return on capital} = \frac{\text{Net profit}}{\text{Capital}} \times 100$$

$$= \frac{£2.5\text{m}}{£20\text{m}} \times 100$$

$$= 12.5\%$$

$$\text{Net profit margin} = \frac{\text{Net profit}}{\text{Turnover}} \times 100$$

$$= \frac{£2.5\text{m}}{30\text{m}} \times 100$$

$$= 8.3\%$$

These figures could be compared with those of another business in the same industry or those with the previous year. This will help you to evaluate their performance.

key terms

***Financial ratio** - a calculation involving two financial figures that are related. They are used to evaluate the performance and financial position of a business.*

***Spreadsheet** – a method of storing data in cells in such a way that a change in one cell will automatically change any other related cells.*

portfolio practice

A toy store has been expanding. The number of stores it operates in the last three years is shown below.

Year	2001	2002	2003
Number of stores	98	110	122

(a) (i) Calculate the percentage increase in the number of stores between 2001 and 2002.

(ii) Calculate the percentage increase in the number of stores between 2002 and 2003.

(b) When did the biggest increase occur?

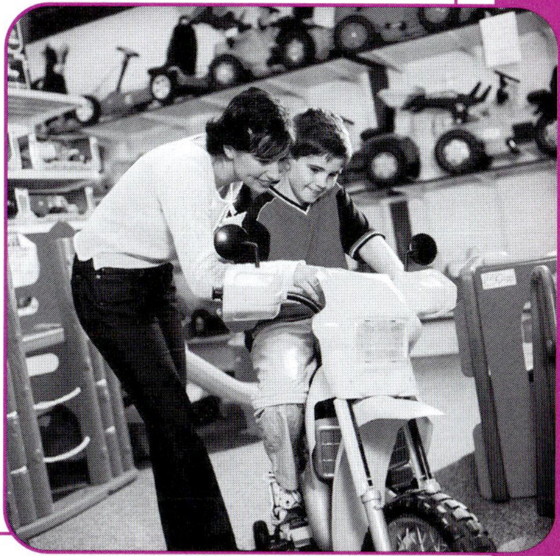

13 Making oral and visual presentations

Making presentations

You will need to give a least two oral presentations during the course. This involves talking to a teacher about some information that you have collected and prepared. You may also have to talk in front of other students or visitors. Below, Linda Jennings is giving a presentation on the customer services provided by Premier Computers, a local supplier of computer hardware.

Linda is using transparencies on an OHP to show the audience some statistics

Linda is standing up positioned at the front and looking at her audience

Linda is using notes to help remind her what to say

Linda uses a video and other material to support her presentation

Practise your skills

State three things that Linda would have to do before giving the presentation.

Preparation

The success of a presentation will depend a lot on the preparation. The first thing to do is draw up an action plan. The action plan here shows the steps Linda Jennings used to prepare for her 15 minute presentation.

- Linda decided to use some information that she collected from Premier Computers on a previous business visit including a short video given to her by the company.
- Linda chose 6 headings for her presentation structure - introduction, delivery, guarantees, callout services, repair services, and credit and payment services.
- Linda wrote just over half a side of A4 for each heading.
- Linda prepared seven OHPs. For each of the headings above she had a list of bullet points. The seventh OHP was a table with some data about customer complaints.
- Linda spent a lot of time reading through what she had written. She wanted to be able to talk without reading from a script.
- Linda practised the whole presentation in front of her sister. It took 17 minutes.
- Linda decided to cut down the amount of time she spent on the introduction. She thought it was a bit drawn out. She only showed the video for one minute instead of three.

Action plan

Objective

Prepare a 15 minute presentation on the customer services offered by Premier Computers.

Deadline

16.12.03

Tasks	Complete by
1. Gather information	2.12.03
2. Choose a list of headings for the structure	4.12.03
3. Write an account under each heading	9.12.03
4. Prepare OHPs for headings and data	11.12.03
5. Learn the written information	13.12.03
6. Practice the whole presentation in front of sister	14.12.03
7. Make changes if necessary	15.12.03
8. Give presentation at 11.00 am	16.12.03

Review

I thought the presentation went well. I was nervous to start with but they seemed to go after about a minute. My OHPs needed to be a little clearer. People at the back couldn't see them properly. I also needed to spend more time practising. I had to look at my notes a bit too often.

Tips on reducing nerves

Most people get nervous when giving a presentation. This is quite normal. The following tips might help to keep your nerves under control.

- Thorough preparation. If you know what you are doing there is less to worry about.
- Practise your presentation first in front of a friend, a relative or even the mirror.
- Use some visual material. This diverts attention away from you to the image.
- Get to the room early. Check your notes and equipment and set yourself up so that you are comfortable.
- Ask if you can have a glass of water handy. Taking a sip might help you to remain composed.

Practise your skills

Describe briefly the sort of things Linda might have talked about in her introduction.

Visual material

Although a presentation is about talking to an audience, it is a good idea to use some visual images. These will make your presentation more colourful and interesting. You could use one, or a combination of the following. Note that Power Point and Interactive Whiteboards can also be used for visual presentations. These are covered in section 14 of this book.

Transparencies for overhead projectors

These are often used in presentations on an overhead projector (OHP) to show headings, bullet points and statistics. So they are sometimes referred to as OHPs.

Posters

These can be used to show a range of information such as diagrams, bullet points and statistics. Posters can have great impact because they can be made large.

Photographs

These can be used to support information that you are presenting. Photos of people and production facilities may be useful.

Handouts

You may put extracts or all of your presentation on a handout. This allows people to refer back to what you said at a later date.

Physical or promotional material

Product samples or wrapping materials might be interesting for the audience to look at and handle. You might also use promotional material from the company to support points.

Video material

Short film clips of interviews or business activity can add a lot. However, they must not be over used, perhaps two or three minutes in a 15 minute presentation. You would need to arrange to make use of video and a television in your classroom. Alternatively you might show the video clip on a computer.

Preparing OHPs

One method that could be used to prepare an OHP transparency is to use a word processor and copy it onto an acetate. Clip art could be used to add some pictures. It is also possible to produce hand written OHPs using felt pens. Whichever method you use OHPs must be clear and bold. Colour will improve their quality. The OHP here was used by Linda.

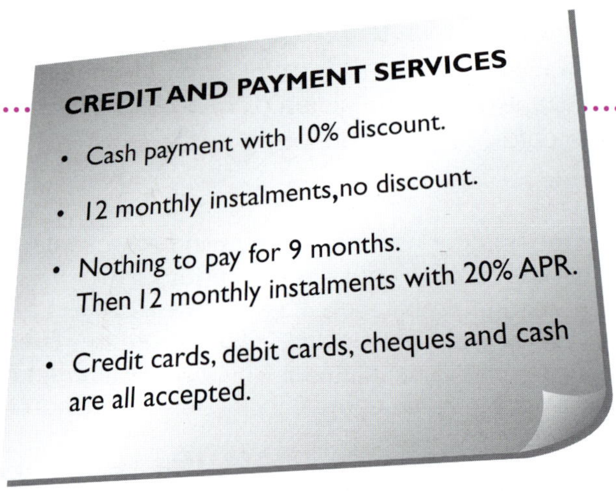

Practise your skills

Produce an OHP transparency outlining the advantages of using visual material in presentations.

Advantages of using presentations

- Presentations can be interactive. For example, members of the audience can ask you questions. Or you can ask the audience questions. Information that you are giving can be clarified and supported with further explanations.
- Making a presentation allows you to talk more and write less. You will be assessed on what you say, not just what is written down.
- You are likely to become more confident after you have given several presentations. This will help you in other areas, such as going for a job interview.
- It may be more interesting to receive information from an oral presentation. People may remember more easily something you have said than something you have written.

The DOs and DON'Ts of presentations

DOs

- ✔ Dress smartly. If you look good, you will feel good and this will help you to perform.
- ✔ Introduce yourself and your presentation formally.
- ✔ Speak clearly. Project your voice to the back of the room.
- ✔ Make eye contact with members of the audience.
- ✔ End your presentation with a clear summary of the main points. Invite questions.
- ✔ Keep to time.

DON'Ts

- ✘ Try not to read everything from a script. This will make your presentation boring.
- ✘ Don't sit down. Stand at the front where the audience can see and hear you.
- ✘ Don't rush what you are saying. Speak deliberately and normally.
- ✘ Don't write lots of text on an OHP. Visual images are for impact, not detail. It can be difficult to read from far away.

Evaluation of your presentation

A teacher will assess the quality of your presentation. The feedback given to you can be used to improve future presentations. Keep a copy of the evaluation statement. You should also review your own presentation. For example, note any ways that you could improve in the future. Finally, you should also keep the action plan, notes and any visual images. They may be needed as proof at a later date.

portfolio practice

Prepare an action plan for a presentation on the different methods of written and oral communication that are used by two businesses. You have three weeks to prepare for the presentation.

14 Using PowerPoint and Interactive Whiteboards

What is PowerPoint?

Many computers have an application called POWERPOINT. This is a computer program that is designed to create slide shows that help to show your ideas in a visual way. This could be used to improve the quality of presentations to different audiences and make them more interesting. PowerPoint allows you to include:

- pictures, photos and artwork;
- tables and charts;
- sound, media and video clips;
- animated images;
- narration;

alongside the text information that you are presenting.

For a PowerPoint presentation you need to have a computer available on which the material to be presented is stored and loaded.

For example, you may be presenting the main findings of the research you have done on two contrasting businesses for Unit 1 to your class. Your teacher says that you can use either over head projections (OHPs) or a PowerPoint presentation. By both methods you can show the ideas you want to get across clearly on 'slides'.

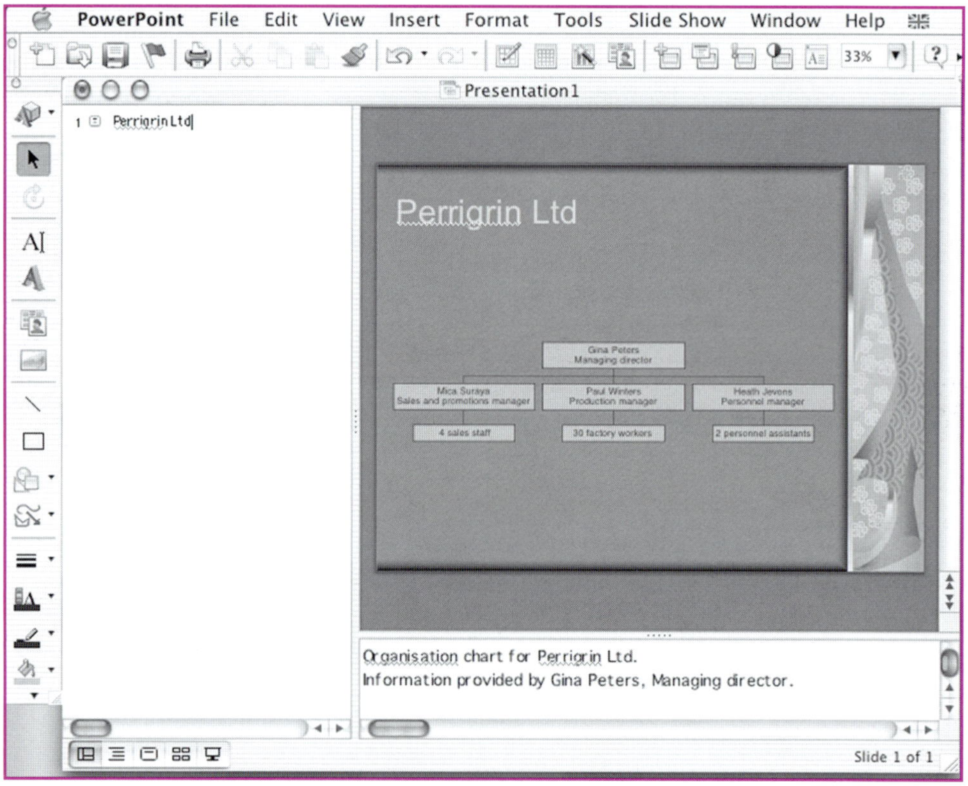

However, with a PowerPoint presentation you can use more varied illustrations to help make the messages more interesting. You can design a 'slide show' which puts over all your information in a positive way. The work that you have created on the computer can be directly communicated to your audience without having to create OHP 'slides'. You can also make use of moving images and sound, and include video images.

Practise your skills

Identify two advantages and two disadvantages of using PowerPoint to make presentations to your class.

Preparing an effective PowerPoint presentation

How you might use PowerPoint for a presentation on a business that you have researched for Unit 1? You have been asked to present the following information about the business to the class.

- The name of the business.
- The goods that it produces.
- The type of business that it is (retailer, producer, distributor).
- The type of customers it aims its products at.
- Its main competitors.
- Its aims and mission statement.
- The way staff are organised into departments.
- Where it is located and why it chose that location.
- How it uses ICT.
- How it provides a service to its customers.

You will have all the information that you need from your research. You will now need to turn it into a PowerPoint presentation. You might create the following slides on the computer.

Slide 1 The name of the business, including any logos if possible. You could ask the audience if they know the name of the company from the logo. You can then add the name to your slide by animation.

Slide 2 Show a photo of the products or a moving image of people using products and ask the audience if they recognise them.

Slide 3 Highlight the business's position in the consumer chain, perhaps as a moving image.

Slide 4 Show the markets for each of the products and who buys them. The business may provide some statistics on age groups that are buying various products, for example. You could show this as a graph or table. You could manipulate the graphs to illustrate changes.

Slide 5 Show logos of the major competitors of the business and ask the audience to identify them.

Slide 6 Show the mission statement of the business.

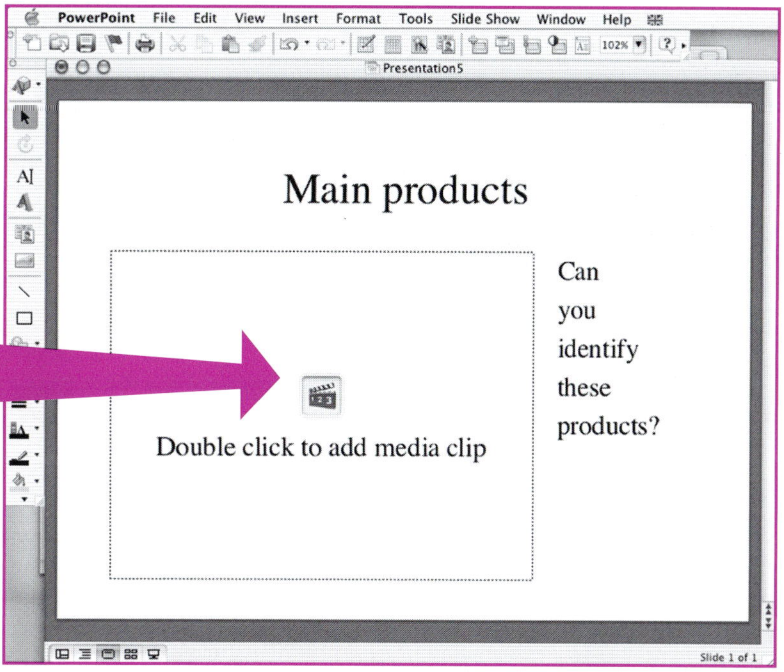

Practise your skills

Complete the slide show above by describing the possible content of a further four slides. They should cover the remaining areas that you have been asked to research. Remember to show how you might illustrate each of the slides.

Tips for producing a good PowerPoint presentation

- Know precisely what it is you are trying to communicate to your audience, for example your findings about what a particular business does or sells.
- Structure the presentation in such a way that all points have a logical order. For example, there is no point starting to tell the audience about how profitable a company is, then moving quickly onto human resources and then coming back to the company's balance sheet. This will only confuse the audience.
- To assist with the impact of the presentation you may want to include some special effects, known as 'animation'. You can make your titles and key bullet points swoop in from the left or right of the screen or appear like a blind being opened. You can also have pictures or symbols emerge suddenly on the screen at the end of a slide.
- Keep the audience involved. Use interesting graphics that get their attention or things that they recognise. You could also ask them questions such as whether something is true or false.
- Always practice your PowerPoint presentation on your computer before you present it. You can then make sure that the slides are all in the right order, that the 'animation' works and that you will be able to cover everything in the time available.
- Don't try to put too many words on each slide. It is useful to use bullet points.
- Try to make the slides as varied and interesting as possible. Use as many ways of presenting information as you can, including text, pictures, still images and moving pictures.

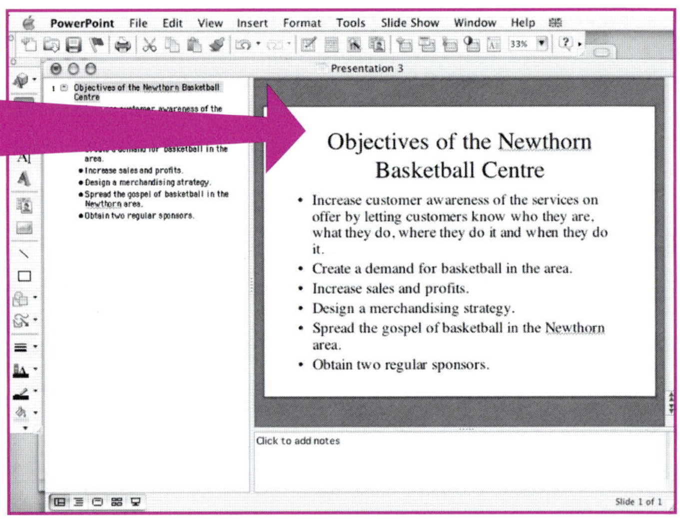

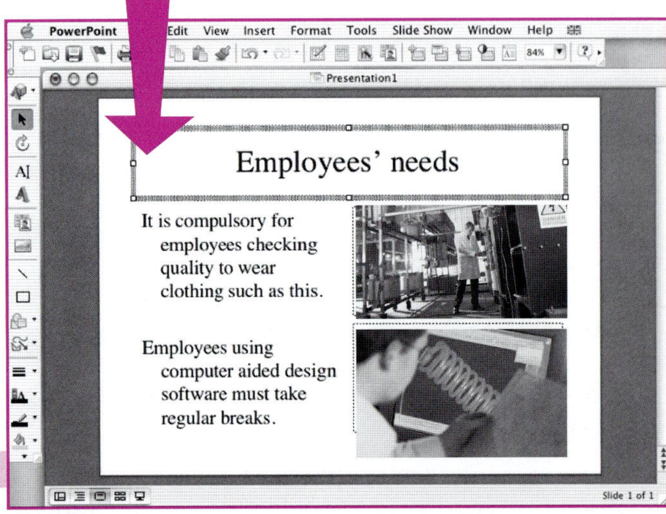

Using an Interactive Whiteboard

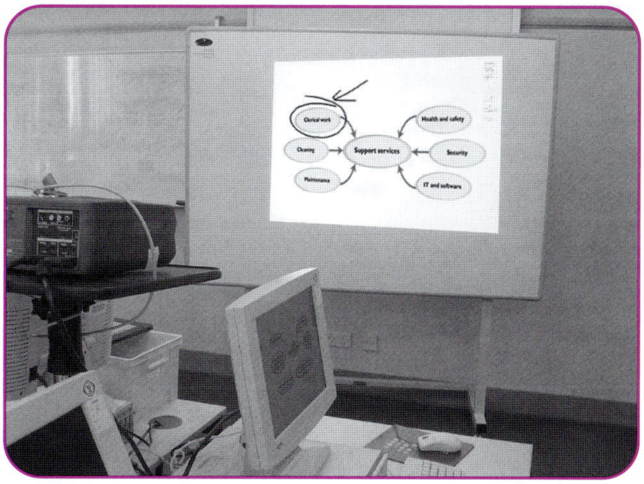

PowerPoint presentations are often made by projecting a computer screen onto an OHP screen. This requires you to use a projector as well as a computer and you have to control the presentation by using the mouse on your computer.

An INTERACTIVE WHITEBOARD will allow you to control your presentation more directly. Interactive Whiteboards are electronic whiteboards which can be used like a large computer screen. By linking your laptop to a whiteboard, you can control your PowerPoint presentation by tapping particular parts of the board with your finger, a pointer or pen. You can point things out using arrows or circles and make links between parts of your presentation all on the Interactive Whiteboard.

For example, a cash flow forecast might be prepared as part of your PowerPoint presentation. This is then projected onto the Interactive Whiteboard. You could then quickly fill in costs and revenues and demonstrate how it might affect the business next year. In order to keep a record of what is written, Interactive Whiteboards can also be linked to a printer so that what presenters show on the board can be printed out.

key terms

PowerPoint - *a computer application which is designed to help you to improve the quality of your presentations to different audiences and make them more interesting.*
Interactive Whiteboard - *electronic whiteboards which can be used like a large computer screen but which allow you to record new ideas or make changes as you are making a presentation or explaining a point.*
Animating a presentation - *the process of putting in moving special effects into a presentation to make it more eye-catching for the audience.*

portfolio practice

You have been asked to produce a short PowerPoint presentation on the ways in which a business you have visited recruits and trains its staff. You have been asked to cover the following topics.

- Methods of advertising for staff.
- How staff are selected.
- The legal rules that affect recruitment.
- The different types of training used.
- The costs of training for the business.
- The benefits of training for the business and the employee.

Outline six slides that you could use to cover these topics, and say how you would illustrate or present each slide to make the presentation interesting.

15 Writing reports

What is a report?

Much of the information in your portfolio can be presented in REPORTS. A report is a written document. It is used to communicate information formally. You can use reports to show what you have found out during research or investigations. The report will contain a written summary of the important information. Below is an extract from a report written by a researcher for the local radio station Crash FM.

TO: The Programme Manager of Crash FM
FROM: Sonia Collins – Media Research Ltd
TITLE: An Analysis of the Morning Show Listeners
DATE: Tuesday 22nd October 2003

Introduction

Listeners were interviewed in three major towns to find out their opinions of the Jude and Alicia Morning Show.

Main findings

- The 11 – 18 age group found the music too dated and the chat too boring.
- The 18 – 30 age group listened mainly in the car and wanted more news and travel spots.
- The 30 – 50 age group liked the music but did not like the chat.
- The over 50 group only listen by mistake.

Recommendations

- If you want to get more listeners, produce a programme aimed specifically at the younger age groups.
- Decide if you want an information show, an entertainment show or a music show.

Practise your skills

Read the report on Crash FM.
(a) Who likes the radio show most?
(b) Who dislikes the radio show most?
(c) What should the producer do about the Morning Show?

What are reports used for?

Reports are common in business and everyday life. For example they are used by:

- schools to tell parents how well pupils are doing;
- work experience supervisors to say what a pupil has learnt on a work placement;
- garage mechanics to show what repairs are needed for a car;
- plcs to tell shareholders how well the business is doing;
- business consultants to make recommendations to their clients. For example, a consultant may recommend that a client needs to train the workforce.

Reports are used to communicate information in a simple way. Information is broken down into 'easy-to-read' parts. This helps the reader to quickly get a picture of what the information is about. Reports are often used to help make decisions. For example, some shareholders may decide to sell their shares after reading about the poor performance of their company in the Annual Report and Accounts.

Reports often have a structure which makes them easier to follow. A business report will start with a formal section showing:

- what the report is for;
- who has written it;
- the title;
- the date.

Introductions

An introduction will explain briefly what the report is about. It may also say where the information has come from. This is a short section and you shouldn't write more than a couple of paragraphs. The example here is for a report on credit control at Wickson's Ltd, a sheet metal supplier.

How does IT improve credit control at Wickson's Ltd?

Introduction

Wickson's Ltd uses IT to monitor customer payments. I spoke to four staff in the department to find out how IT speeded up customer payments. I also asked them how the performance of the department was measured.

Practise your skills

Look at the extract from Neil Johnson's school report. What is the purpose of this report?

Subject: Business Studies **Name:** Neil Johnson

Date: 18.12.03 **Attendance:** 98% **Grade:** A

Comment

Neil has made a great deal of progress in this subject. He is enthusiastic, hard working and a lively member of the class. He has developed some good research skills and has a high standard of presentation. Next term he will need to spend more time practising analysis and evaluation.

Well done!

Signed: T. Sanderson

Main findings

This is likely to be the longest part of the report. It is used to explain what has been found out during the investigation. It will contain a lot of analysis. It is common to divide the main findings into a number of sections. Each section should have a clear heading. Also, each section could be broken down into sub-sections. Each sub-section may be a single paragraph. The example here is an extract from the report on credit control at Wickson's Ltd.

Section heading

Sub sections

> **Main findings**
>
> **Aged debtors schedule**
>
> Wickson's prints out an aged debtors schedule at the end of every month. This is a list of customers that owe the business money. The customers at the top of the list have owed money for the longest.
>
> The aged debtors schedule is used by Wickson's to target slow payers. Customers who have owed money for more than 3 months are targeted. Personal visits are made to these customers by the head of credit control.
>
> Since using the aged debtors schedule bad debts have been reduced by 22%.

Conclusions

A report will usually end with a conclusion. This will be a summary of what has been found linked to the aims of the research or investigation. It is a very important part of the report. It will contain a lot of evaluation. This involves making judgments about the main points raised in the report.

> **7 Conclusions**
>
> IT has helped Crafton plc to improve its credit control for the following reasons.
>
> 7.1 IT provides up to date information about how much each customer owes.
>
> 7.2 IT warns Crafton if customers try to go over their credit limit.
>
> 7.3 IT produces an aged debtors list which identifies customers that have owed money for too long.
>
> 7.4 IT sends out reminders automatically to customers who have forgotten to pay.

The example here is an extract from a report into the use of IT at a different company, Crafton plc. The writer has decided that IT has helped the company to improve credit control. Reasons for the decision are given in the conclusion. Note that this report has numbered its headings and sections. This is sometimes used in formal reports.

Practise your skills

Look at the extracts from the report on the use of IT in credit control at Crafton. Explain why numbering the sections might be useful.

Recommendations

Sometimes reports are used to make recommendations. This involves the writer saying what the business should do after analysing the findings of an investigation. Again this section will contain a lot of evaluation because judgments are being made. The example here is an extract from a report on recruitment and selection at Pinfold Ltd, a medium-sized pet food manufacturer. The purpose of the report is to suggest improvements to documentation and procedures.

Recommendations

Reduce the size of the application form from 6 to 4 pages. It currently takes too long to read each form.

Design an evaluation form to record information about interviewees during an interview.

Give out more information about the company at interviews.

Increase the length of interviews from 15 to 25 minutes. 15 minutes is too short.

Ask more open questions at interviews. This will encourage interviewees to talk more.

Appendix

Some reports will need an appendix. This may contain basic data, questionnaires, calculations, notes and references. Such detail should not be included in the main report. The purpose of a report is to present information concisely. Tables of data, notes and calculations will clutter up the report. This is also dealt with in section 16 of this book.

Tips on report writing

1. Plan your report before writing it.
2. Draw up a list of headings and place them in a logical order.
3. Gather together all the information you have researched before you start to write your report.
4. Make your report attractive by using graphs, diagrams, pictures and other visual material.
5. Don't include any irrelevant material. Don't be afraid to leave things out.
6. When your report is finished you can number the pages. Then add a list of contents, but only when you have finished.

key terms

Report - *a written summary of all the information that a business or person has collected. It is used to help make a decision.*

key terms key terms key terms key terms

portfolio practice

You are planning to compare a large fast food restaurant business and a small roof repair business. Plan out the main headings for a report. Write briefly what would be under each heading.

16 Organising, sorting and indexing

Contents

Your portfolio will be handed in for internal assessment. You should aim to make a good impression. It will help if the portfolio is organised, indexed and neatly presented. This makes it easier for teachers to assess. You should include a contents page. This gives a summary of the information included.

The extract shown below is the contents page for Unit 1 from Lewis Small's portfolio. He has investigated two businesses, Vodafone and Andy's Cafe. The contents page shows titles of the work he has done and page numbers.

CONTENTS

Unit 1 Investigating business	**Page**
Introduction	1
Vodafone and Andy's Cafe	
1. Scope of activities	3
2. Ownership	5
3. Location	7
4. Aims and objectives	10
5. Functional areas	14
6. Relationships between functional areas	21
7. The use of IT in the functional areas	24
8. Internal communication methods	26
9. External communication methods	30
10. How might communications be improved	33
11. Notes on my oral presentation	36
12. External influences – competition	39
13. External influences – environment	43
14. External influences – economy	46

Your introduction should not be too long.

Page numbers should be shown clearly.

The titles of all the work in your portfolio should be shown in full.

You might decide to have contents pages at the beginning of the portfolio or at the beginning of Unit 1 and also Unit 2.

Collecting and storing data

The work in your portfolio will be based on information that you have gathered from businesses and other sources. You will need to store this information for a period of time. You could keep data in envelope files, perhaps one file for each business that you investigate. Examples of data that you might collect include internal business documents, Annual Reports and Accounts, computer printouts from the Internet, photographs, pamphlets, drafts of work that you have done and diagrams.

Practise your skills

Describe briefly why it is important to present your portfolio attractively.

Organising your portfolio

Your portfolio might be presented in a ring file. It will contain work for two Units - Unit 1 Investigating business and Unit 2 People and business. It might be a good idea to keep the work for each unit in a separate section.

Unit 1 Investigating business

In Unit 1 you have to investigate two contrasting businesses. One method of organisation is to have a section for each business. This is shown on the left hand side below. The two businesses are Abdul's Sweet Centre, a sole trader, and Tesco, the large supermarket chain. The four topics for assessment (A, B, C and D) are covered for each business in each of the sections.

Another approach is to use the one shown on the right hand side below. Here the file is divided into four sections, one for each topic area A, B, C and D. In each section work for both businesses is filed.

Unit 1 Investigating business

Abdul's Sweet Centre

A Activities, aims and objectives, ownership and location
B Business organisation and functional areas
C Communications
D External factors

Tesco

A Activities, aims and objectives, ownership and location
B Business organisation and functional areas
C Communications
D External factors

or

Unit 1 Investigating business

A Activities, aims and objectives, ownership and location
Abdul's Sweet Centre
Tesco

B Business organisation and functional areas
Abdul's Sweet Centre
Tesco

C Communications
Abdul's Sweet Centre
Tesco

D External factors
Abdul's Sweet Centre
Tesco

Unit 2 People and business

You only have to investigate one business for Unit 2 so organisation is made easier. The example here shows the section divided into five areas.

Practise your skills

Suggest three reasons why it is important to organise your portfolio effectively.

Indexing

Your portfolio will contain a lot of work. Therefore you are advised to INDEX your work. This will help readers to find particular pieces of work without having to search through the whole file. It will save time.

When you index your work you will need to number all the pages in your portfolio. However, you should leave this until you have finished all work. This will avoid having to change all the page numbers if you decide to move even just one piece of work.

The example here shows indexing for Unit 2. Readers are guided to the information they are interested in by the page reference.

CONTENTS

Unit 2 People and business	**Page**
Introduction	1
Scottish & Newcastle	
1. Stakeholders	3
2. Job roles	5
3. Working arrangements	7
4. Contracts of employment	10
5. Employers' rights	13
6. Employees' rights	17
7. Health & safety	21
8. Resolving disagreements	25
9. Recruitment	28
10. Job applications	32
11. Training	36
12. The importance of customers	38
13. Customers' expectations	45
14. Customer satisfaction	48
15. Customer service	54
16. Protecting customers	59
17. Appendix	
(i) Copy of handbook	62
(ii) Interview notes	64

Appendix

You might use an APPENDIX. This involves putting information such as tables of statistics, business documents and raw data in a separate section at the back of your portfolio. The information placed in an appendix must not be essential to what you are writing about in the text. For example, you may be discussing customer services in Unit 2 and refer to some comments made by customers in a survey that you did. The actual comments made by customers during the survey would not have to be shown in the text. They can be placed in an appendix. The reason for using appendices is to avoid having too much unnecessary information in the text.

Practise your skills

State which of the following information is likely to be placed in an appendix. Explain why you would put these items into the appendix.

1. *A detailed map of a business's location.*
2. *A graph showing how profit has fallen in the last 5 years.*
3. *Questionnaires from a survey on working conditions.*
4. *A pie chart showing the market shares of all the businesses in a particular market.*

Bibliography

You could write a BIBLIOGRAPHY at the end of your portfolio or each Unit. A bibliography is a list of all the sources that you have used to produce your portfolio. The list will include the sources you have used for background information and for your research, such as textbooks, journals, company information and magazines.

Examples might be:

- textbooks, eg *GCSE Applied Business*, D.Hall, R.Jones, C.Raffo. D.Gray, edited by I.Chambers & J.Dickinson, 2003, Causeway Press, Ormskirk;
- newspapers, eg *The Guardian, 22.7.2003, Guardian Newspapers Ltd*;
- company information, eg J.Preston, Managing Director, Nettles Ltd, St.Ives, Cornwall.

Tips on improving presentation

- You should make every effort to word process all the work in your portfolio. If you do choose to hand write your work then it must be very neat.
- Make sure that all spelling and grammar is correct. Use a spell check on the computer or ask your teacher for help with difficult words and grammar.
- If you include graphs, diagrams and charts you must refer to them in the text.
- It is important to label and title all graphs, charts and diagrams clearly.
- The use of colour in diagrams, graphs and charts, for example, will help to brighten up your work.
- The work inside the ring file should not be put into plastic file slips. This is unnecessary and makes marking more difficult.

key terms

Appendix - *information added on at the end that may contain further explanation but is not essential in the main text.*
Bibliography - *a list of sources used to produce a lengthy piece of written work.*
Index - *a guide to help the reader find information.*

portfolio practice

(a) Make a list of all the stationery that you will need for the organisation and presentation of your portfolio.
(b) Why is it important to refer to all graphs, diagrams and charts that you use in your portfolio?

17 How your portfolio is assessed

Assessment

You will get more marks for your portfolio if you understand how it is going to be assessed. Marks are awarded for certain skills. Therefore you need to demonstrate these skills when producing work for your portfolio.

The assessors will be looking for three particular skills. They are called ASSESSMENT OBJECTIVES (AO).

AO 1
- Demonstrate and apply business knowledge.
- Show that you understand business terms, concepts, theories and methods.
- Use business terms, concepts, theories and methods to address problems and issues.

AO 2
- Plan and carry out investigations of issues by gathering, selecting, recording and analysing information.

AO 3
- Evaluate evidence.
- Make reasoned judgments.
- Present conclusions.

Tips on earning more marks

- Make sure your work covers the assessment objectives.
- Get your teacher to check work before finally putting it into your portfolio.
- Always back up any statements you make that show knowledge, analysis or evaluation with evidence.
- Units 1 and 2 carry the same amount of marks. So spend roughly the same amount of time on each unit in your portfolio.
- Don't be afraid of making judgments and giving opinions. There may not be a right or wrong answer.
- To show evaluation clearly use terms like 'In my judgment...', 'In my opinion...', 'In my view...', I think that...', I would argue that.....'.

Practise your skills

The extract shown here is from Unit 2 in Sheila Hand's portfolio. She is describing the job role of one of the staff at Winecare Ltd , a wine wholesaler.
(a) Which of the three skills do you think is being demonstrated in this extract?
(b) State three business terms that are used in the extract.

Eric Williams is in charge of marketing at Winecare Ltd. His main role is to provide detailed monthly sales figures for senior management, organise promotions and ensure that distribution runs smoothly. He also deals with customer complaints and designs incentive schemes for sales staff.

Knowledge

To demonstrate knowledge you have to show that you understand the business environment. You can do this by using business terms appropriately in your work. The business terms in the examples here are shown in bold.

BUSINESS TERMS

- Haircare Ltd used **market research** to estimate its **market share**.
- In the next **financial year** NFT's **turnover** fell but **gross profit** rose.
- Cassons' **buying function** is **centralised**. This helps it to achieve **economies of scale**.
- When **interest rates** fell **demand** for cars picked up.

You will also have to show that you understand business concepts and theories. Business concepts are the ideas or notions about running business. Theories are rules or laws that explain what is likely to happen in a particular business situation. Some examples of each are given here.

CONCEPTS

- Worker specialisation.
- Just-in-time manufacturing.
- Total Quality Management.

THEORIES

- When price is increased demand will fall.
- Investment in new technology will raise productivity.
- During a recession cash flow problems may increase.

You will also get the opportunity to demonstrate knowledge when addressing business problems and issues. Two examples are shown here. The business terms are shown in bold.

PROBLEMS AND ISSUES

- **Customer complaints** at BankCorp might be reduced if **external communications** are improved.
- **Growth** is a **business objective** that might benefit a wide range of **stakeholders**.

Analysis

ANALYSIS involves breaking down (or dissecting) the information that you have gathered. It also involves understanding and explaining what the information means. You will have to analyse both numerical and written information. You can demonstrate analysis in a number of ways.

You can try to find links between different bits of information. You might decide that there is a pattern in the information, for example. Or you might find that one event described by the information is a possible cause of another event. Some examples are given here.

LINKS AND PATTERNS

- The graph shows that when staff turnover rises productivity falls.
- Revenue may be rising because the price has been cut and demand has increased.
- Sales may have fallen because staffing has been cut in the customer services department.
- Communications may be poor because the computer system keeps breaking down.

You can use mathematical techniques to analyse numerical data. For example, you could use ratios to analyse financial information such as balance sheets and profit and loss accounts. The example shown here uses break-even analysis to see whether a business has met its aim.

MATHEMATICAL TECHNIQUES

Betty hoped that her business would break even after one year. During the year total costs were £89,000 and total revenue was £74,500.

Unfortunately, since revenue is £14,500 (£89,000 - £74,500) less than costs the business has failed to break-even. Therefore her aim has not been met.

You can use business theories to help explain patterns and events in the information. The example here uses exchange rate theory.

BUSINESS THEORIES
Between 1998 and 2002 Warwick Engineering suffered a loss of overseas customers. This could have been due to the strong pound making UK exports more expensive.

Practise your skills

East Anglia Motorcycles has been established for 20 years. It sells motorbikes in Norwich. At the end of 2001 a new competitor entered the market selling bikes cheaply from a warehouse.

What links are there in the data?

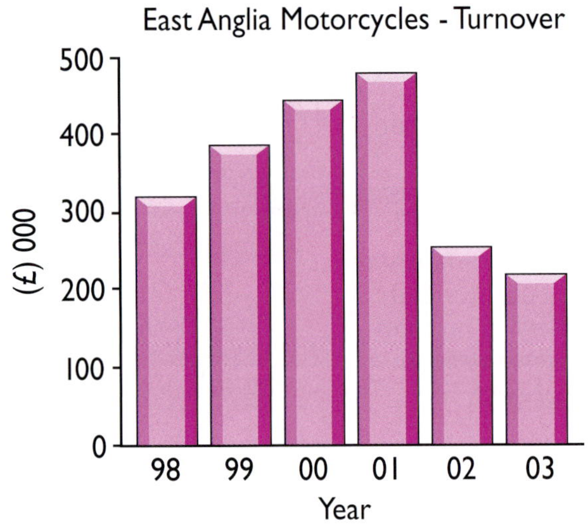

Evaluation

EVALUATION is probably the most difficult skill to demonstrate. You need to show that you can make decisions and solve problems based on the information that you have gathered and analysed.

One way to demonstrate evaluation is to be selective when using information. You need to show that you can recognise the difference between useful information and useless information. Here the student has recognised that information on interest rates is of no use.

INFORMATION SELECTION
The graph shows that interest rates in the economy have been very low in recent years. However, sales of dog food would not be affected by interest rates. Therefore low interest rates cannot be a reason why sales have increased.

You must show that you can make judgments based on the information you have gathered. You may need to weigh up a number of points and make a decision based on what you think is right. Here the student is deciding whether a business should invest in refurbishment.

MAKE JUDGMENTS
I think Toni Sartori should refurbish his restaurant. The cost is high and cash flow would be tight. He will also have to shut for a month. However, he will be in a better position to compete with a new restaurant that has just opened and it will provide a chance to relaunch his business. He could take out a loan and shut down in the winter when its quiet.

You will have to draw conclusions from the information that you have analysed. Again this involves weighing up the main points. Drawing a conclusion usually involves giving an opinion based on the data. Here the student is deciding why staff motivation has fallen.

DRAW CONCLUSIONS
I think staff motivation has fallen because communications have broken down. The new manager is too isolated. She never speaks to staff face to face. She doesn't keep them informed about the firm's progress. All she does is put notices on the canteen wall. I don't think the recent pay freeze is as important as communications.

Assessment marks

Assessors award marks according to what level you have achieved. This means that more marks are awarded for more detailed answers. Detail is linked to the amount of analysis and evaluation you show. Consider Unit 2, People and business. The table below shows that up to 3 marks might be awarded for simple descriptive answers that demonstrate knowledge. A further 3 marks might be given for analysis. Finally, more detailed answers will contain knowledge, analysis and evaluation. A further 4 marks might be given for evaluation. The table tells you what to do at each level to gain the marks available. This is an example. The mark scheme could be different depending on your course.

KNOWLEDGE	ANALYSIS	EVALUATION
Identify the stakeholders in the business and describe how the business affects them.	Explain how stakeholders influence the business.	Explain how conflicts between stakeholders arise and suggest how they might be resolved.
Unit 2 0-3 marks	**4-6 marks**	**7-10 marks**

Below is an example for Unit 1, Investigating business.

KNOWLEDGE	ANALYSIS	EVALUATION
Identify the main external influences on two businesses.	Explain the impact on two businesses of changes in external influences.	Suggest and justify the ways in which two businesses could respond to changes in external influences.
Unit 1 0-5 marks	**6-9 marks**	**10-12 marks**

key terms

Analysis - *breaking down or dissecting information to find out what it means.*
Assessment objectives - *the skills that need to be demonstrated in portfolios.*
Evaluation - *making judgments or recommendations and drawing conclusions from evidence.*

portfolio practice

Recently there has been an increase in the number of people that work from home, for example, writers, journalists, sales staff, consultants. Some say that developments in ICT have increased home working. With ICT people can keep in touch with what goes on at work. Some businesses like their staff to work at home because it saves a lot of money. Another view is that home working has grown because manufacturing has declined. Other reasons include changes in the way parents share in the care of their children, more female workers, less manual work and more self-employment.

In your view, what is the main reason that has led to the increase in home working?